go
and
preach
no
more

a legacy abandoned
my life reclaimed

William Raff

Foreword by Leonard Ostrander

Think First Publishing
Los Angeles, Ca

Library of Congress Control Number: 2024923454

ISBN: 979-8-9918487-0-1 (Hardcover) | ISBN: 979-8-9918487-1-8 (eBook)

ISBN: 979-8-9918487-2-5 (Paperback)

Edited by Barbara Ardinger Ph. D

Cover designed by Getcovers

Think First Publishing

Contents

For my parents
who only wanted the best for me.
And for those of you who come after me,
I wish you the very best that life has to offer.

The Common Man

Undistinguished common sameness
From darkness into the light of his mother's eyes
Celebrating twofold joy.
Uncommon joy.

Elbows and knees a tatter
A kiss on a salty cheek, celebrating
Unconditional love.

Hormones grip, possess him,
His heart, tortured by a kiss, denied.
Undeniable pain.

Whiskers sprouting, a cautious smile in repose
Fingers crossed; what prosperity comes from
Common undistinguishable sameness?

The man who sprang from
Aaron Copland's distinguished pen,
Brass and timpani, exulting
A Fanfare to the Common Man.

—Wm Raff

Foreword

As the president of The Clergy Project since 2018, I am perhaps something of a subject matter expert (SME) on lives salvaged from the destruction caused by religion and subsequently rebuilt on the more durable and productive foundations of human values, science, and reason. I have witnessed a swath of destruction, far more devastating than natural disasters, ironically called acts of God, which leave entire communities destroyed in their wake.

There is no easy way to speak to the ruined ambitions, ruined lives, and ruined families, that have resulted, when brave men and women, former religious leaders, and respected members of their communities, speak their truth, a true moment of revelation for them and an end to their crisis of faith which then results in an apostate, of whom I am chiefest among them. With apologies to Mac Davis, wherever you are, it is indeed hard to be humble when you're apostate in every way. I can't wait to look in the mirror, because I get more apostate each day.

Every story I have heard from survivors like Bill is unique. But I can relate to every one of them. It begins with absolute conviction and a strong need to serve, to believe, to battle doubt. No one fakes such dedication. This endures right up to the end, when we are dragged "kicking and screaming" (Bill's experience) from a life of faith into the brighter light of verifiable truth, reason and humanist values.

What is not unique is the devastation that follows when we share our new reality. None of us leave unscathed. Many are left broken and abandoned by our closest friends and family. Divorce and shunning are all too common.

But the good news is that religious leaders who no longer believe and whose lives are all too often left in ruins by the lies of religion are not without hope.

Wm Raff, (Bill) the author of "Go and Preach No More," is proof positive that it is possible to negotiate life without a god. Bill is a true survivor of religious indoctrination and an obscure denomination of which I knew very little.

Bill's demanding work in writing this memoir is a gift to us all. Sharing knowledge is one of his passions and he does so with a most endearing style.

I encourage you to tag along on this exciting journey with him. From a place where he could say that "Christ and the Gospel now held the most prominent place in my revamped world," to stating his appreciation for "the benefits of being a non-believer."

His is a memorable story of hope and encouragement to us all wherever we find ourselves on the road of life.

All of us, Bill and I included, who have found solace in The Clergy Project (https://clergyproject.org/) owe a debt of gratitude to Dan Barker, Richard Dawkins, Linda LaScola and Daniel Dennett for founding and opening the doors to a community we so needed.

The Clergy Project is a community which has grown out of a shared struggle. For our participants, that is truly good news, far better than the message we came to reject when we courageously questioned our beliefs and challenged the myths we once taught. If you question our bravery, consider what we've risked and lost.

Here's some more excellent news. If your point of view is from within the church, if you are looking out, looking for escape, consider that a little doubt and the willingness to question even the very existence of the god of your own childhood indoctrination, are more than adequate to separate you from the imaginary love of an imaginary god, and the debilitating baggage that superstition brings.

The Clergy Project is a one-of-a-kind online community that exists "to provide support, community and hope to current and former religious leaders who no longer hold supernatural beliefs." To accomplish our mission, we offer the following services from a secure and confidential website dedicated to our members' needs. It begins with a multi-topic online forum, allowing each member an opportunity to share their personal story and offer support to one another, to share needs, projects, and ideas. That community also flows into a closed Facebook page which hosts lively conversations and plenty of humor but can instantly rally when a friend hits a rough patch. Also on the website, members can inquire about counseling through the Secular Therapy Project. And for those who have found it difficult to transition out of clergy related employment, vocational counseling is available. Those who find the need for greater anonymity are free to use avatars and pseudonyms to protect their privacy.

Yes, you read that right. Our community of over thirteen hundred apostate religious leaders, hailing from fifty nations around the world, were all atheists when we applied to join The Clergy Project.

We refer applicants who are undecided or still experiencing a "crisis of faith" to our good friends at Recovering from Religion (https://www.recoveringfromreligion.org/)

While positive outcomes and happy endings are not guaranteed, we at The Clergy Project are fortunate to hear many success stories. We have escaped or are in the process of escaping from the bonds of dozens of world religions and scores of Christian denominations.

Leonard (Lon) Ostrander,

President of The Clergy Project

If you would like to know how the Clergy Project came into being, Bill has been kind enough to share our story in Appendix 6.

Author's Note

I have not been part of the Christian community for the last twelve years. One thing has remained sure: I never have, nor will I, regret the friendships formed in the church I grew up in or the church which welcomed me in after I left my childhood faith. Those memories remain a cherished part of who I am.

The amazing times we shared together, like someone once said, are for me, A Moveable Feast. I will continue to savor its bounty for the rest of my life.

My story and how I tell it, is as I remember it happened. It makes sense that you may not remember my version. And why should you? We all see life through our own lens, even though we may have been in the same room with the same people at the same time. Those details are subject to the patina of time, which leaves its own subtle trace on our lives. This is what's known as recall bias. Please take this into account as you reflect here.

Since I left Christianity in 2012, I have led a quiet life. When I thought a conversation with an old friend would benefit from an update, I gladly shared my new belief. Otherwise, I saw no need to advertise it. I did not write this book to proselytize anyone or argue for a cause. I do share why I now believe as I do.

A memoir, the genre I use to tell my story, requires a single theme, a thread that stretches from cover to cover. Which is why I tell the story of my religious journey and all its requisite baggage. I felt my Christian journey, memoir worthy; and I wanted to commemorate its significance in my life.

I have made my peace with the individuals and the ideas that I disagreed with, and using a historical approach helped me maintain that peace as I told my story. I made my own choices and harbor no rancor, having willfully given my life to that cause. And I respect those who continue to do so.

I am more content now than I have ever been, and I wish you the same in your endeavors.

P.S. In the print versions of this book, you'll find a page of QR-Codes at the end of the Appendices. Use the camera on your mobile phone and the QR codes to go directly to all the links in this book.

Preface

A personal story, your own story, can change a life and deserves to be told. I would add that the best way to know a person's story is to hear them tell it themselves. This is the main reason why I have decided to share mine. For some of you, my story may serve as a warning, for others, an admonishment; or it could serve as an inspiration to listen to the voice in your own heads and celebrate its unique agency.

A decade after my father passed, when my mother was packing her belongings to move from Boise to northern Washington with my sister and her husband, she sent me a text saying I should expect a surprise in the mail. A week later, I held a bulky manila envelope in my hands and wondered what she had found. I opened the envelope and pulled out a half ream of typing paper. I immediately recognized my father's handwriting and admired both the patience it takes to write in cursive and the clean practiced style of his hand, thinking to myself that I was glad I had learned to type.

The first sentences I read suggested it was an autobiography. This grabbed my attention. Eager to share some time with my old man, I made some coffee and settled into my favorite easy chair. Five pages later, I flipped to an empty page and some major disappointment followed. Why my mom had included a half ream of empty pages I can only guess. The story those yellowed pages teased me with, and the layers of memories I was hoping to find between them, would, after the disappointment, become the fuel I needed to write this book.

Remembering the rush that took hold of me, that swell of hope I felt when I first saw my dad's pages, I decided that I would find a way to leave a full accounting of my life for my own children. I don't expect it will have the same effect as that package did on me, since I have been boasting to them about writing my own memoir for over three years now. Maybe when they are my age they will look back and set aside some time to reminisce with their old man. And if you do sit down from time to time, and travel in my shoes a bit, bring with you the wonderful memories that only we as a family could have made, and sprinkle them between the scenes I've used to paint my story.

The process of getting this book in front of your eyes has been quite challenging. I am a person who tends to read instructions. I like to literally follow a recipe and can become quite frustrated if I can't find the exact ingredient specified. So I paid attention to the advice I found for new writers. I researched, designed, and built an ergonomic writing space. That was the easy part. One piece of advice that made sense to me convinced me to create a memoir that not only my family but also a general audience would find interesting. In the process of preparing to write, I acquainted myself thoroughly with the concept of what a memoir is. It's not an autobiography, and, as such, I realized there was only one theme that might carry enough interest to appeal to a general audience. In my case, it was the religious thread that runs through my family, beginning with my grandparents, all four of them, who, before they were married, individually became a part of the same international church.

My paternal grandfather became the leader of our church in California. My father and four of my uncles, then my brother and I would all dedicate substantial time as ministers to the same cause. In my case, my parents all but preordained me while I was still in the womb. That religious lifestyle would challenge me at several points along my journey and some sixty years later, the word "atheist" would define the man who emerged from the fray. A happy atheist, I might add.

I did not write about my journey with the intention of discouraging anyone's belief in God. But it is an integral part of my story to share how my curiosity eventually won out over the strong beliefs I once held and promoted. If that offends you, I apologize, and you won't hurt my feelings if you decide to set my book down now. Or just trust that your faith is immutable as I once thought mine was.

Prologue

One of the most astonishing perspectives I acquired while in college is the ability to consider time, all time since its inception, in the same way one takes in a mural, in this case, a mural spanning fourteen billion-years, the approximate age of our universe, and to do so from a point in time that allows me to compare my lifetime of seventy years relative to that expanse.

This perspective was a gift from an astronomy professor at the community college I attended. Both the universal timeline and big history[1] could be considered synonymous, reducing a lifetime, my seventy years, into a microscopic blip in time.

History was one aspect of life that captivated me, beginning in junior high school. Throughout my life, I've used it as a lens through which I could consider the events and people that paved the way for my life. History, whether spoken or written, allowed me to stop and look back and forth in time and observe how others made their way. I noted how the actions of others affected me and considered how my actions might

---

1. Big history presents a picture of what happened over the expanse of time starting at the moment of the Big Bang up to our current place in time, roughly 14 billion years later. Based on scientific calculations, it predicts such things as where on that timeline light first appeared or when modern humans evolved on earth.

determine my own future and the futures of those I loved. History could be considered a time machine of sorts.

One thing that any time traveler is keenly aware of is his or her point of origin, which represents the place where all that we know, all that we cherish and hold dear, exists and intersects with our lived life and in so doing is marked (like parentheses) by a fixed time of birth and an imagined time of death. From this perspective, what may seem like a long life is reduced to a little blip. And each blip can also be further reduced into smaller divisions: years, weeks, days, and seconds. The idea of relativity then becomes a curious thing to ponder.

Can you, as a person, relate to the age of the universe in any meaningful way? Does it make you feel small or insignificant in any way? Or does it excite you as it does me?

The story I'm about to share with you will not reveal why I find both dogs and cats to be worthwhile and interesting pets. Or that I love to cook or any of a hundred other details about my life. The thread I will weave begins before my birth and continues right up to this moment as I type these words. And one never knows how a few words can find their way into the future.

The common theme that has extended over those seven decades is how I have framed my existence on this earth, how I have seen myself relative to the mural I describe here, and to the concept of big history that I speak of. As we all know, we come to exist having no say about the color of our eyes, our preference for vanilla or chocolate, or our gender...'tis a long list. We have no point of reference to define our existence until we see the light of day. And then there begins a series of experiments. What does the world sound like with our eyes closed? What does the world feel like if you are born without the ability to hear? Another long list. Each of us has a slightly different point of reference to which we must learn to adapt.

My challenge upon birth was to learn to fathom my world using an ancient laboratory. The test tubes and beakers in my case were filled with hope, faith, and religious dogma. The scope of my inquiry was meant to inform my purpose and existence based on ideas that ancient sages and prophets had conjured thousands of years before my birth, or based on the inclusive scale of big history, just a few seconds ago (relative to 13.8 billion years). This was the grand experiment to which I was challenged to dedicate my life. At the time of my birth, my parents believed that this option held all the answers to every question I might have about life and the journey ahead of me.

Remember the mural I spoke of in the first sentence? Imagine you're in a museum. There's a bench in the middle of the room, far enough away from the mural on the wall to allow you to take in the breadth of the universe, a span of 13.8 billion years. Have a seat and let the significance of this masterpiece come over you. Consider the vantage point that bench offers you. (That bench could be described as any place on our planet where an individual, having the skill and access to a telescope, might observe the universe.) When I set aside my parents' religious concept of the universe to consider another option, I observed how the idea that God, from his first appearance in a man's dream and every tale attributed to him since, fit right into that same tiny blip.

During my education I learned about brilliant people who'd made use of thought experiments to understand the universe we live in. I followed their example and set up my own thought experiment. This book is the story of my lifelong quest for the truth about who we are relative to our place in that great span of stars and galaxies. As such, it is my story, my concept of life.

I challenge you to find your own answers and hope your answers bring as much satisfaction to your life as I now enjoy. But for now, welcome to my world.

Part One

The Legacy

1

God's Mustache

Old enough to meet God

Sounds of gravel underfoot, locomotives champing at the bit, pressure valves erupting. All a blur now on the sepia print in my head. The dissonance which toyed with my three-year-old brain made me squeeze hard on the adult finger leading me to our passenger coach. Even now, my gut churns when a sense of danger overwhelms my instincts. I don't much care for things that make me feel small or shatter my peace at night.

Now when I go back in time, I think more lyrically of that train depot, its obstacles, its charm. I imagine the concatenated iron stretching from one ocean to another, reaching out, connecting bright cities, and on their journey, seamlessly woven across our glorious land, gliding over purple mountains' majesty and past amber waves of grain. That if you touched the cold steel at any point; all at once, you became part of Los Angeles, Chicago, and every treasure in between.

Dad, Mom, and Grandma Charlotte were setting out on a pilgrimage with a three-year-old boy in tow. I did not understand that the looming adventure was a part of my indoctrination into a cult-like belief and that it would have significant sway over my future. The man we were going to see believed, like his followers, that he was God's Representative on Earth.

Johann Bischoff was coming from Germany to Chicago, and we were going to sit at the feet of this great man. My mother would have pointed to his prominence in our home as the date for our pilgrimage to meet him approached. He watched us from a photo in a narrow black frame that hung on the wall of our living room. His gray mustache looped like a roller coaster at the ends of closed, neutral lips. He always wore a black suit, a white shirt, and a black tie.

Years later, Grandma Charlotte would tell me about the great sorrow in her life that accompanied her to Chicago. She had been widowed quite young and was not invited to attend that Saturday evening's service for active ministers and their wives. She shared how she wept that night. Her only solace had been to care for me, her first-born grandson, while my parents attended the service. Had her own Bill, my grandfather, and an Elder in our Church, still been alive, she would have been sitting at his side.

Men like Bischoff had formerly frequented Grandma's home because her husband had been a somebody in the Church. They had sipped coffee together while Apostles and Bishops, the men having the greatest authority in the church, expounded on God's plan. Playing the parts of both Mary and Martha, Grandma had kept the coffee hot and her heart open to these spiritual messengers. Heaven is present on earth when faith is everything in your life.

Johann Gottfried Bischoff was *der Stammapostel*, the Chief Apostle of the New Apostolic Church.[1] Awe-struck ladies would cup their hands over their mouths if this man walked within ten paces of them. People referred to our church as the German Church when I was a boy because immigrants, including my grandparents, imported its doctrine to America.

I would notice later in my life how everyone acted differently when preparing for visits from men like Bischoff. The local leadership pecked at subordinates to get everything just right. Neckties straight, every folding

1. See Appendix 4

chair placed perfectly, a warbling soprano or inattentive tenor chided. The heightened stress cascaded down every rung of that authoritative ladder, stating the obvious. God was coming to visit.

My parents and I arrived at the hall in plenty of time to get a good seat. I have no idea how long we sat, or how many times my mother leaned over to remind me we were in church, to be good, to be quiet. A toy would have kept me occupied on the train, but this was not a train. We behaved ourselves in church, which translated for a three-year-old into boring.

And then the mood changed. All of those practiced, local choirs, rising up like molehills to form a great mountain. As they pushed off from their noisy steel chairs, not one chair was left straight, a startling tremor quickly followed by silence. All the singers' eyes were now fixed on the baton, and every soul in the hall was anticipating greatness, and then...goosebumps! Even as a three-year-old, I knew something wondrous was happening.

The rush repeated itself when, after the choir had prepared the congregation for the service with several songs, the entire hall fell silent again and then with a mighty chord, the organ summoned all the thousands of believers that had traveled here to their feet. The great pipe organ's riffs and the unison of voices welcomed the guest of honor.

And there he was, that handlebar mustache up close. But I would not make it through his sermon, which was translated into English. I fell asleep, my head on my mother's lap, while her eyes were faithfully focused on God's Servant speaking at the altar, which was no longer just a piece of wood; it now represented God's embassy on earth. Stern-faced ambassadors flanked it, their eyes fixed on the Rock upon which Christ once told Peter he'd build his Church, now my Church, now built upon the faith of one Johann Bischoff. I know that because I would learn to attach the same significance to the successors of those men among whom I would walk one day. My people and my mother had told me this would happen.

After the preaching and singing, the last prayer and the benediction, a rousing organ interlude brought my people to their feet. We sang the threefold amen. My fist on sleepy eyes, I heard a blur of voices crescendoing on each amen and the harmonies assigned to them. And that was the closing parenthesis of the serious part of the service.

Then, more words. There's only so much a three-year-old can take, and I was ready for some fun. But the adults were still in Heaven, and they crooned and swayed in ecstasy. I remember laughter, too, a pretty girl presenting a bouquet to the Chief Apostle, and then a last song, "Till we meet, till we meet, till we meet at Jesus' feet." The bass voices would growl the "till we meet" while the others held the final note. This song brought tears to every eye except those of us kids who had not yet fully understood what we had been born into. As an adult, the unifying spirit of that song would move me to tears as well.

Somehow, after the song ended and the adults realized the service was over, I escaped my parents' watchful eyes. I was found wandering behind the stage by a man who would add a significant quantity of excitement and grief to my life a decade later. This man lifted me into his arms and walked to the front of the stage, where he announced that he'd found a curious boy. Would his parents like him back? I have little recollection of the moment. I may have been terrified or in tears or just glad to see over the entire crowd, which was bustling in conversation. It was probably my first glimpse of such a mass of people from a vantage point I would know better someday. The man's name was Michael Kraus. He was an Apostle from Canada.

Although I was only three, many of the highlights of this adventure would stay with me my entire life. Subsequent events would reinforce my sense of belonging. The connection which I felt as a little boy, and which continued throughout my adult life would some day complicate my life as does gravity a rocket struggling to leave this earth.

After my parents reclaimed me, there was more to endure. The ritual of shaking hands with all the ministers and the Chief Apostle could take hours for all in attendance-to touch the Hand of God. Belief in God was second to the belief in the men and the authority they claimed as Ambassadors of Heaven. This was Rule One, the very essence of the dogma of our Church. We were all taught the importance of looking up to those chosen men. What began literally, continued figuratively when we became adults. God demanded it.

2
Counting Rafters
A preacher's kid ~ pirates ~ and a water cooler

Imagination offers a magnificent virtual stage to all ages. It may be to blame for all the gods we curious *sapiens* have conjured. Imagination can become a secret friend to converse with, a library to ponder in, or an exotic paradise in which to play the pirate. As a child, I was a daydreamer and frequently set off exploring in my head while the preachers droned on. While I counted the rafters overhead in the church, sometimes I would hear something that would make me wonder…what were these adults going on about? Or I slept on the wooden seats because sometimes while my parents were at Saturday night meetings, we had stayed up late the night before watching Perry Mason or Lawrence Welk while Grandma dozed.

Church attendance was a given, a part of normal life and as constant as a heartbeat. We had to attend three times a week, whether in sickness or in health, but if we kids were seriously ill, Mom would stay home with us. Complaining did not help us, as much as it confirmed to my parents that they were teaching us longsuffering, a fruit of the spirit and a vital tool for life's journey. There was always some challenge, and usually something I made a fuss about, that Mom would insist I endure. I remember, for example, having a strong aversion to short pants and scratchy sweaters, the only kinds available when I was a kid.

There was plenty of mischief to get into before and after the service, though during the sermon mischief was nearly impossible. No one would dare misbehave. But seeing our cousins and friends was worth enduring such indignities in church or out. This was our only social circle; it was my village.

Sunday morning kicked off a day of chore-free possibilities. Sunday School, held before the service, went in one ear, out the other. Sermons, like I said before, were a time to imagine being somewhere else. Pick a stage, cast the characters, sharpen your sword. After Sunday School and before the service, our large old church building and its grounds became a virtual gameboard. Scaring each other to death in the basement storage room was always good cardio and strangely fun. That old curtain covering the door...if it caught on your suspenders and held you back—yikes! Or, if one of us ran ahead and hid, popping out from between the old furniture piled up in there—boo! Terrifying! We'd run back up the stairs, imagining monsters on our heels. Out of breath, we'd line up at the old water cooler behind the vestibule. (When we were growing up, we didn't know that room had such a fancy name.) When we'd had our fill of water, every chin dripping, our wet ties and shirts often prompted a comment from the nearest adult: "Hey, what you all been up to?" Cue the giggles. "Um, bye!" We'd take another lap and meet back at the watering hole ten minutes later. A few of us led the brigade, and the rest made chase.

Sunday afternoon service, now that was a harder pill to swallow. A major interruption after Sunday dinner, which almost always included cousins or company. Sometimes company meant we had to behave at dinner and, worse yet, sit and listen if a minister wanted to talk Church before dessert. Sitting still for more preaching could chafe considerably when all we wanted to do was play in the yard. Only half the members present in the morning service came to the 5 p.m. service, which, as I got older, gave me plenty to think about. Why did we have to go if others could stay home? What annoyed me most was why the leadership kept insisting on that custom. My father used to say that church members voted with their feet. Meaning, if they didn't like something they knew they had zero say-so about, their feet either took them out the door to another life or refused to take them to church on Sunday afternoon. My feet were never given that choice.

Once a month, the Sunday afternoon service was called a children's service. I think it was a riff on Art Linkletter's show, *House Party*, later known as "Kids Say the Darndest Things." In our church, the minister would come down from behind the altar and get us chatting. (The altar was still just a piece of furniture to me at that age.) We sat up front where the choir usually sat. He'd stand in front of us kids and lean in close like a friend. I can still see his compassionate smile and his wavy silver hair. We called him Uncle Carl, but he wasn't one of my real uncles. Uncle Carl was also an amateur magician and finished each children's service with some magic tricks. We had to stand when answering a question, and sometimes I guess I got too nervous. I remember sharing a Sunday dinner with Uncle Carl, my stomach erupting and my lunch ending up on his pants and shoes.

Wednesday's service started at 8 p.m. Before we were old enough to stay awake for the whole service, and because all the free babysitters (i.e., aunts and grandmas) were at church, we were "tucked-in" on the pews. My dad, who was an assistant priest (aka associate pastor in most faiths), sat to the side of the altar. One night, he left his seat during the service and came down from the podium. It turned heads, but one of us kids was snoring. He got half-way to the back of the church with his cargo before he realized he'd grabbed the wrong kid.

As we got older, and too big to carry, Mom or Dad would wake us when the service ended, and we'd know it was time to go to the car. One night, when my brother got the tap to wake up, he went out to our car to resume his dreams. Except it wasn't our car. The church was in a residential neighborhood, and he got in the back seat of the neighbor's car by mistake. And as if that wasn't bad enough, the neighbor needed to go somewhere and drove off with him. The man was very upset with my dad. It was bad enough that so many cars crowded his neighborhood three times a week, and I guess finding a strange kid in his backseat was just too much to handle.

A couple times a year, the Apostle would visit our area. It was a big deal. In those days, travel was challenging. He lived in Chicago and would spend a week in our district. On Saturday night, his first service was just for the ministers and their wives. (Grandma would babysit us at home.) Sunday morning was a district service when all the congregations in Los Angeles came together in one place. (My home congregation at Highland Park served as the district church until we outgrew it.)

The week of the Apostle's visit meant a week of travel for our family because the Apostle visited the outlying congregations around Southern California, one per night, and we would show up for each nightly service. To do this, we'd pile into the car as soon as Dad got home from work.[1] Each night was a road trip. If we had to go all the way to Fresno, dinner would be a picnic in the car. Each morning, Dad was off to work, and we went to school, but when we got home, it was off to San Diego, San Bernardino, Fresno, or some other city. Each night after the service, we'd stand in line to shake hands with the guest of honor. Crazy, you say? Yeah, today I'd say traveling those distances on a school and work night to see the same person

---

1. The majority of ministers in the NAC were not paid for their service but had secular jobs or businesses.

each time made our lot unique. But dozens of families whose fathers were ministers joined this caravan two or three times a year.

My dad once told me the FBI visited our services during World War II. I'm sure it was standard procedure back then to ascertain if such a concentration of German citizens posed any threat to U.S. interests during wartime. That didn't stop German members of our proud village from conducting sermons in their native tongue, even a decade after the conflict ended. There were lots of German members who'd pounce on anyone speaking German in a supermarket or on a bus. My dad referred to their tactics as test-a-fighting, their version of "testifying." (Or proselytizing, which at the time, meant insisting our church was the only way into heaven.) That's how the church grew in the United States, German members insisting their church was the *scheisse* (the shit - in English). For years, I heard our church referred to as the German church.

I am a third generation American, and when I was a boy, the Church still catered to those that only spoke German or preferred hearing a service in their native tongue. Mom, who was the organist for that service, took me with her on those Thursday nights. I imagine Mom and my grandmas hoped that speaking German would rub off on me. So, she plunked me down in the last row under the watchful eye of Uncle Donald (also not a real uncle). He was the deacon in charge. We had this tête-à-tête going, he and I. I'd scratch out percussive codes on the wooden seat with my buzz cut, my message: I don't want to be here (which I hoped Mom would understand too). In return, he would thump me on my head like he was shooting a marble. I would eventually enjoy learning the language and to this day I enjoy watching German TV and films online.

My dad and his family had moved to Los Angeles from Brooklyn, New York when he was a kid, and the Church had tapped his father to become the next District Elder for the West Coast. (Although Grandpa would have had a choice, no minister would have turned down such a commission and I rather suspect he and Grandma jumped at the chance to live in California.) That made my family a kind of royalty in our congregation, seen from a kid's eyes. Many members remembered my grandfather and shared stories of his investment in the growth of the Church in California. I never got to meet him, though. Both of my grandfathers had bad kidneys and died in their early forties.

Even though we had plenty of fun at church, my entire family, including the ministers and Sunday School teachers, teamed up to define the difference between the social perks of "fellowship" (common slang in many churches for gathering after a service for food) and the serious business that God and his Servants conducted there, which they defined in black and white terms, the very colors worn by all ministers and choir members when at church. As a child, I was expected to accept this difference at face value. No questions asked, not out loud anyway. We kids had marvelous meals and treats down in the same basement we played in, and those moments were filled with laughter and my favorite *kuchens* (Grandma Kroner's *Strueselkuchen*, or crumb cake). Upstairs in Church, however, it was emphasized that man did not live by bread alone, but by every word that God spoke. And God spoke at Church through His ambassadors, the Apostles. This serious business was telegraphed through the solemnity of the service and the pious looks of the adults attending, those I knew could laugh and tease with the best of us, but not while frozen in that serious mindset.

I never had to "open wide" for supplements like castor oil and vitamins, but Mom held more sermons than Dad ever did at church. Every day, like a mother hen, her religious view on life hovered over us. Suffice it to say, a reverent cloud hovered over my entire childhood. Whether we were at church or at home, it made its presence known.

When I was seven, an unusual event touched my life, and not in a good way. I would travel through life quite a while before its significance and implications would become crystal clear. It began on a run-of-the-mill Sunday morning, when the minister cut the sermon short and asked my father to read a letter to the congregation.

My Aunt Elsie was sitting in the pew next to me. When I remember the details further, my mind supplies different information. It's not terribly important to this story, but it's a clear message to us humans that our memories do overlap and easily interchange facts. I know that we sat behind the choir that day, but my memory is not clear if we sat on the new solid benches or the old folding, theater style seats. The raw end of this story is the recurring anxiety which twists my guts into a knot whenever my mind perceives an existential threat. When your aunt cries out in grief and adults all around follow like dominoes, a little boy takes notice. My gut told me something exceptional had happened.

Ministers often used the term "stumbling block" in a sermon to describe a test of faith. The week before that day in 1960, the head of the church worldwide, Chief Apostle Bischoff died. The news was devastating, especially because on Christmas day, 1951, he had proclaimed that Jesus would return during his lifetime. At the age of seven, I could not comprehend how the hubris of his prediction followed by his death, i.e., proof he had been wrong, could affect the faith of an international church that was entirely focused on one thing: the Second Coming, always called the First Resurrection.[2]

---

2. Revelation 20:5 KJV: But the rest of the dead lived not again until the thousand years were finished. This *is* the first resurrection.

Of course, the faithful would provide explanations. My mother always favored the saying "Everything happens for a reason." While this is an excellent premise to apply in physics, I never found it useful to offer to people who were going through difficult times.

The mantra for that generation, which was gob smacked by Bischoff's *faux pas?* "As for me and my house, we shall serve the Lord." A week later, the head of each family in each congregation was polled during special services. "Will you pledge loyalty to the next Chief Apostle?" Most did, and life went on. A few members checked out, but my clan doubled down.

Not all things in 1960 would be so earth shattering as the Chief Apostle's death. Both Grandma Charlotte and I would have good fortune. She would marry a handsome minister from New York, the first man I would call grandpa. And, in Detroit, a baby girl would be born, my future wife. It was not, however, a good year for our church.

I'm not sure when I first felt that my childhood was just taking too long. Something in me, most likely the natural inclinations of our species, was pushing up on the soil of childhood just eager to break through the surface and bloom. Those urges morph and squirm in a young mind that is constantly being reminded of its place in nature and by God.

Elementary school was my first introduction to the "world" as presented by the Church as a place to be wary of. I believe I found school interesting because I have always been curious about life, but I carried a premonition that evil lurked nearby. Besides that, I was constantly reminded that we were supposed to be and act differently from other kids. It would be my first introduction to an elitist attitude that maintained a wedge between me and my peers until I graduated from high school.

While I felt the urge to sow my oats as I grew older, I also felt the shackles that emphasized my religious heritage and calling in the Church. While I had no idea what my future held, I knew great things were expected, probably because my mom was always whispering in my ear. She imagined wonderful things for me, and these things all included serving God, which I assumed included all the perks that went with service: a ministry, a wife (often referred to as a helpmate) and a career adaptable to service.

School was like trudging through thick, wet snow. Not literal snow, as I lived in Los Angeles, but as something I needed to endure to acquire all the perks of adulthood. I believe all children are competitive. Some are in-your-face gamers. Others, like me, are plotters and schemers waiting for the right moment to pull ahead and snatch the prize. In a large metropolis, the cliché is to hurry-up and wait, whether on the freeway or in elementary school. The illusion that life is picking up speed, and that growing up is within reach, is just that, an illusion. In future musings, I would ponder chaos theory, the idea that something as insignificant as the beat of a butterfly's wing could alter the course of history. I'm not sure I'll ever decipher every word, frown, or lesson that nudged my life through the maze that was my childhood.

3
Rapids and a Waterfall

Just go with the flow ~ Easy for you to say

Questioned by his parents about his unsanctioned whereabouts, Jesus, at the age of twelve, responded that he needed to be about his Father's business. I'm not sure my dad would have accepted that for an answer from me when I was that age. Rules were rules. When I was twelve, the church leadership decided twelve-year-olds could join the choir. This was a rare opportunity to pull ahead, as I was also nearing the confirmation age of fifteen.

I, too, wanted to be about my father's business. It seemed to be in my blood.

I remember an aunt providing me a bit of rope to climb up to my goal when I insisted I could help in the kitchen and peel a potato. Does it count if a little skin ends up in the dinner? I had this notion I could do anything the adults were doing. Maybe better. And joining the choir was my chance to prove it. I'd have to wait until after confirmation to join the youth choir, but there were still two choirs I could join.

The local congregational choirs had always been a crap-shoot. Well-meaning conductors let the spirit move their arms with the same abandon observed during the wave at Dodger Stadium. The members of these choirs could seldom read music, and a gaggle of warbling female voices competed with each other, using their voices to self-righteously elbow each other out of their way, and the tone-deaf competitor was always ready to return the favor. The tenors and basses either knew what they were doing and accepted the pandemonium or simply kept their heads bowed in their hymnals, where they would remain throughout the entire selection. It's a wonder they knew when to sit back down. Of course, I always took notice when a choir and conductor proved me wrong.

Our district choir, however, was a reputable group. This I knew already at age twelve because I had developed an ear for fine music while listening to the local classical music radio station. Every Saturday evening, my father listened to the same program. He had this beautiful German-made radio that was the size of a suitcase. (Its polished, contrasting wood grain may have also influenced my love for woodworking.) Dad would press an ivory-colored preset, adjust the volume, and while listening to the music, he'd begin preparing the sermon for the next day. I absorbed the exceptional harmonies, and while listening to those voices soar and harmonize, wondered if our choirs would ever make me feel like I was in heaven the way they did. I estimated that we had eons to go.

Herr Nieter, a gentleman who, along with his wife, I heard, sang opera in Germany prior to immigrating to the United States, conducted our district choir. While I imagined them singing the duets and arias I'd hear on Dad's radio, it could have been that he and his wife sang either in the chorus of an opera company or just at college. She did have a stunning soprano voice and often sang solos. Herr Nieter's deep, commanding voice rolled off his tongue, his soft German accent lending old world authority to his instructions. This choir practiced once a month, more if an Apostle was planning a visit. My guess is that there were probably a hundred voices, possibly more, as we filled the entire annex of the district church, which was my congregational home base. (A monthly district service, combining all the congregations in Southern California, brought members from as far south as San Diego and as far north as Fresno.) I could soar with those musicians twice a month. I don't remember Herr Nieter using musical jargon to guide us during practice because his words would have fallen on deaf ears. Years later, a young music major would take our youth choir to new heights when he insisted, as our conductor, that we all learn to read music.

I still remember my first district choir practice. It was like walking among giants. Inclusion in adult activities like the district choir was a tremendous boost to my ego. It was around this time that I was also teaching myself to play the piano. I played by ear and could not read music, but I had memorized many hymns. My playing also made me feel good about myself. It was part of my DNA, a primary tool that allowed me to express my faith.

At twelve years old, I was noticing my life picking up speed like a river leading to a waterfall. Swirling in the currents below a challenge called out to me: to accept my future as an adult in the Church. To accomplish this, I would need to commit to the dogma of the Church and bend to the wishes of my elders who had charted out my life for me. It was what I'd told myself I wanted, to leave behind my childhood and assume my place, my heritage.

I was also coming up with questions that had only one solution, belief, often expressed in the words of the new District Apostle for North America, Michael Kraus: "Childlike belief," which in his mind meant no questions. Trust and loyalty were the only variables in his equation. To him, it was that simple.

There was an inordinate amount of confidence in this man and those he chose to be at his side. If one had difficulty believing in God, these men claimed to have enough faith for themselves and others. It was easier to believe in them than question God. After all, they demonstrated through their actions what trust and loyalty were. Many of them were wealthy and pointed to this as proof that God had blessed them. The faith of my forefathers, which called out to me, combined with my love for music.

These feelings complimented each other and amplified my zeal. It probably helped that my boyish voice was evolving, finding its own timbre, in the lower ranges of the tenor, baritone and, alas, bass notes called for by the music I enjoyed singing.

Now that familiar excuse, "You're not old enough," became, "Get ready now! We're going to be late for...." I was now approaching a time in my life when I could express the faith that my parents and all my relatives, as well as my church family, had been practicing while I merely observed. Singing in the choirs was a big part of that growth. Life was looking up. However, there was one aspect of this growing up that would tie my guts in knots. I was lucky it hadn't happened to me yet.

When my peers and I had ripened to the age of fifteen, confirmation would mark our passage into spiritual adulthood. But, before that, we would be prepared with three years of confirmation classes on Monday evenings. On Tuesday evenings twice a month, we would also attend religious instruction. Now I was going to church almost as often as my dad, who spent three nights a week visiting members in their homes. This was in addition to his Wednesday service and a brothers' meeting on the weekend, all of this after he'd worked his full-time job on weekdays and his part-time gig on Saturdays at a German delicatessen owned by another minister.

While all these changes were happening in my religious life, school and homework also presented challenges. I had a very limited number of "part-time" friends as I progressed through my public education. This was because I did not feel comfortable making friends at school. It could have been my natural tendency toward introversion, or it could have been the religious beliefs I held which I did not feel comfortable declaring. It was probably a little of both.

By the time I was in junior high, I was part of a trio of nerds. We traveled among our peers incognito so we could avoid the bullies that were on the prowl for us weird kids. Some of those bullies were budding gang members and, frankly, they scared the shit out of me. We had also volunteered to be hall monitors, which allowed us to be alone at lunchtime and eat lunch in a stairwell, thus avoiding the general population. We mostly ate quietly, keeping our thoughts to ourselves. Occasionally, we had some interesting conversations about our beliefs. Steve, a carrot top and easily a foot taller than me, was a Jehovah's Witness. He was a good guy to have around when a passerby didn't take to the way he thought we'd looked at him.

One day during lunch I had an epiphany of sorts. As I sat on the cold concrete steps, this nugget of logic popped into my head, which I forthwith adopted: *If there is only one God, then there should only be one church.* (I picked mine.) *And if there is only one God and only my church, then I should dedicate 100 percent of my life to its cause. Amen.* This seemed to be the culmination of the thoughts I'd been entertaining about whether God existed and how my friend's church compared to mine.

As I reflect on this now as an adult, this conclusion was most probably synonymous with my not wanting to disappoint my parents, uncles, aunts, et al. It seemed like an expedient way to settle my deliberations, especially as I saw the metaphorical river of my life picking up speed, and the foam and spray of the waterfall coming up fast.

What stands out now as I look back at that awkward and tumultuous time is the convergence of my coming of age and arrival of the next new leader of the Church in North America, the man about to take the stage. Imagine a thousand-pound gorilla interrupting a church service. When I was thirteen years old, Michael Kraus came to town, and the Church I had known growing up began to change beyond recognition. Already a

District Apostle in Canada, the Chief Apostle added the United States to his territory in 1966.

Religious instruction and confirmation classes introduced my age group to the doctrine, dogma, and history of our denomination. I learned that every Christian denomination that came into existence following the establishment of the Roman Catholic Church has an inciting incident that justifies its purpose and its right to exist in the eyes of its adherents. Our church was no different. And I was about to hear all about it.

The sacristy had always been off limits to children. This was the room where the ministers met before a service, where they counted the offering, where members shared intimate and private concerns with their rectors. It was also the venue for our confirmation classes. I, for one, felt privileged to enter this mysterious room. There were maybe five or six of us if no one ditched.

At the same time, I was nursing a crush. I liked to sit across from her and take in her charms. I remember the large conference table which was shaped like a football with the tips squared off. There, I parked my elbows on the cold, wood grained laminate top, attempting to regulate my lust. Puberty was challenging enough now without the distraction of theological themes taught in holy venues.

After hundreds of sermons, some of which put me to sleep, I was now face to face with the preacher, a.k.a., Dear Old Dad. It was his job to prepare us to become adults in the eyes of the Church. There were several bricks which together formed the dogma and tenants of our belief system. Dad explained these, stacking them together in no uncertain terms. Christ built his Church on Peter's faith. Peter was the first Chief Apostle. The Holy Spirit by way of prophecy called new apostles (in the 1830s) to prepare the Church for Christ's return. Only a living apostle could administer the sacraments, which gave believers access to salvation. Each brick—and those were just a few he used for the foundation—he handed to us as building blocks for our own belief system, our faith.

If we agreed, if we, with our faith as the mortar, assembled the same tenets to match that of the Church, then our faith would be confirmed. Hence the term: Confirmation.

Christmas, and the weeks leading up to the Children's Christmas Program, messed with my guts. For that matter, anything that made me anxious manifested itself with bomber squadrons of butterflies. I suppose all of us kids reacted differently to the challenges of those years. Decades later, as an adult, I would take part in a Christmas musical. The woman who directed the production knew what she was doing and managed rehearsals as we memorized songs and dialogue in a way that eliminated all but a few of my butterflies. But as kids, we were all on our own, squeezing those poems into our heads. The older we got, the longer the poems became. It was pure torture reciting poems in front of adults who thought kids under duress were the cutest things ever. My anxiety and possible stage fright lasted weeks and ended either when I pissed myself or miraculously remembered the last phrase, both of which happened while I seemed to be in a catatonic state. Well, actually, I never pissed myself, but the fear of doing so hovered nearby.

I also remember a doting father in the audience with a set of four flood lights on a stick. He could not hold them still while his movie camera clicked away, filming the spectacle. Confirmation would leave those lights in my rearview mirror. Or so I thought. All I had to do was memorize a small book and the confirmation vow for my ultimate step into sacred adulthood. This differed from actual adulthood, of course, which would have equipped me with the requisite sense and capacity to cut and run.

For three years, hoping I would not disappoint my parents, I agonized about stepping over that threshold of faith. This and other stress-inducing moments now seem an early indicator of our family's history of anxiety and depression. Come midlife, these inclinations would make life more difficult for me.

Religious instruction, another class all faithful adults were encouraged to attend, was also open to children aged twelve and older. In this class, we learned about Christianity's schisms. First, the power struggle that left Constantinople and Rome divided. Then Martin Luther's audacity, which dragged us through the Medieval and Renaissance squabbles between the Protestant and Catholic super-powers.

But the coup de grâce to the traditional church was the Pentecostal outpouring in Scotland during the 1830s. This was what led to our supremacy as the New Apostolic Children of God. It amounted to an edict, the newly formed Catholic Apostolic Church (the first iteration of the last dynasty) declaring its newly minted Apostles as the premier ministry of the End Times. This historical turn included the short-lived rise of this group, whose short-sightedness insisted that only twelve apostles were to be called. When prophets attempted to show those fellas who really controlled the tiller, well, the thirteenth fella called to be an apostle by the prophet, a German, and his supporters, lit out to start his own exclusive club in Germany. The marked success of this splinter group, which called itself the New Apostolic Church (NAC), led this group to eventually gain the upper hand over the prophets, who probably just liked to shake things up a little too much. One does not need a prophet when a perfectly good apostle is available.

By the time my fellow students and I opened our books on the subject, the Church no longer had that new car smell, and the prophets were long gone. But what I learned filled my subconscious with questions. I had a closet for them which could have been labeled *If so, then what?*

Well over a century old by the time I started learning about its roots, our Church had spread to many countries, but not to all. Within the next two decades of my life, though, one enterprising Apostle would invade every nation not yet familiar with its "living apostles." He would export his unique zeal and his custom NAC brand into these lands. That apostle was the waterfall generating the thunder and turbulence of the river pulling me toward the future my mother knew was my heritage. Michael Kraus was the apostle that had found me wandering behind the stage as a three-year-old when my folks took me to Chicago with them.

4

An Exception to Every Rule

It's hard to be a teenage boy without a dogma

I was old enough at thirteen to understand my dad's moods. As Michael Kraus and his expectations invaded our home and congregation, Dad's angst and blood pressure rose. Mom served as a parabolic sounding board as Dad fired off his objections. Unable to help, she watched as his words bounced back, agitating him even more.

Kraus would leave little of our old, *gemutlich* (laid-back) congregation intact. His first order of business was the mandatory retirement of all ministers aged sixty-five and older. This meant that Uncle Carl, our rector, and evangelist, would get the axe. The days of referring to one's "administration brothers" (NAC[1] speak for ministers) as uncles, were also over. Discipline was the new theme. Lines were drawn and respect reinstated. Self-discipline and organizational discipline became the new standards. These changes stressed out plenty of folks in the congregation.

Primed to ascend to my rightful place in the ranks of ministers, I, a naïve thirteen-year-old, now began my induction into the Kraus method. He had many favorite quips, like "There is an exception to every rule." He would make every announcement as a king might, forcefully, confi-

---

1. Pronounced: Knack speak

dently, with a knowing smile. Oh, that smile...it was not celebratory, it was challenging. He dared the congregation to question him with that smile. Because he had emigrated as an adult to the U.S. from Romania, his English would fall apart as he attempted to string longer sentences together in his often-animated state. But the short mantras he had down. Those sound bites he let fly, seasoned with his lilting, signature accent.

I actually enjoyed the shakeup. It was exciting to watch. And the forced retirements took some of the old mumblers off the sermon circuit. A welcome reprieve.

Yes, Kraus was a rule-maker. And like any good rule-maker, he locked in his loopholes. Someone cleverly referred to his rules as "guidelines." His *exception to every rule* pronouncement came in very handy when, only seven years later, his edict regarding retirement hit home when it was supposedly time for him to retire. That "exception" extended his shelf life for an additional twenty-two years and they finally sat him down in his own gilded pew when he was eighty-seven years of age. Legions came out to celebrate his farewell. Once a fan, I would have celebrated his finale too, were it not for the waste of talent and opportunities that had been displaced in his wake.

In his heyday, Kraus' vision for the future seemed grand. Ambitious, driven, inspired, enthusiastic, demanding, feverish—all these were parts of his signature, but as his reign cooled, slowly taking on glacial proportions, new adjectives described him and became less flattering and more derogatory, depending on who you talked to.

In the early days of his reign though, when I was a deacon and then a new priest, I considered him a *force majeure*. This primed me to adopt his visionary zeal. Many mature members were not so sure however, and some of them ran head-on into his stubborn idiosyncrasies. They kicked one gentleman out of the choir for example, because he rejected the new king's methods. They even denied him communion when he insisted on ignoring the dress code. I am still in awe of him and similar figures who, even after suffering Kraus' insults, remained in the church for their entire lives.

Those he called to his side as Apostles "these generals" he called them in televised services—while becoming emotional to the point of distraction, extended his reach around the globe. He had given each great responsibility in the fields he'd assigned to them, but there was no room for criticism of his plan. He demanded a great deal from them, and loyalty was at the top of the list.

You either got caught up in the rushing wind of Michael Kraus or you got thrown wide by it. There was no in-between, especially if you wanted to be a minister during his reign. For many caught up in his charismatic preaching, it was fitting to get a Kraus-cut. Most could not duplicate his silver-blue mane, but they could get their haircut to duplicate the close, nearly transparent sides and back (now called a fade), leaving just enough on the top to lie down with the help of a pinch of Butch wax or Brylcreem. It was a different era.

5
Over the Falls

Wait, what? You want me to preach in front of my friends?

Confirmation day came, and, as with all grand plans, scheduling dictated that the order of things had to change. The examination, usually held the night before, would now take place before the service on Sunday. While the minister conducting the festivities lived in the Midwest, it was either bad weather or good luck that delayed that portly gentleman's flight that Sunday morning. We thirty, somber-faced confirmands from all the Los Angeles metropolitan congregations, busted out in smiles when we were informed that "This year, I will set aside the confirmation examination so that we can start the service as soon as possible." Our local instructors had already assured the District Elder from St. Louis that we all knew that only the living apostles in the NAC could issue a heavenly visa[1] . All we had to do now was to publicly renounce Satan and all his works and ways to get our own heavenly passports stamped for immediate adulthood in the Church. Hallelujah!

Once confirmed, I and my male cohorts were introduced to new challenges designed to test us once again. The most gut-wrenching of these made the yearly Christmas recital look like a walk in the park. But now, this form of torture would be meted out monthly during a service designed

---

1. See Appendix 5

just for the youth, a sort of practice congregation where members of the district youth group, one evening a month, gathered as a congregation of our own. We "newbies" joined other young people (in my day that meant any members not yet married), where we filled all the roles normally needed in a local congregation. Ushers, organists, choir members, and assistant ministers. A senior minister or several were assigned to lead the evening's activities, but we filled the pews and functioned as a congregation on that one evening. Usually just a handful of these "youth" sat in the pews without having another role. Almost everyone was in the choir.

The proverbial deep end awaited those of us who had dreamed about being a part of this group of "cool" adults, many of whom had their own cars, were involved in romantic relationships, and basically were on their way to total freedom from their parents and the restrictions of childhood. But ahead lay the thundering falls: our first and most challenging task was to learn to speak extemporaneously in front of our peers. Half a dozen fifteen-year-old boys, ahem, young men, would be called (each service) to assist the minister by offering Spirit-conjured anecdotes related to his sermon's theme. I do not recall any buffer zone to help us ease into those churning waters. Like an initiation, we were summoned to the altar one at a time.

I remember one fella that just stood there, staring at the building's back wall: a mime expressing the very concept of eternity. When he finally found his voice to say amen, everyone sucked air and chimed in, AMEN! The first time I was called to speak was also memorable, though all I remember now is my fear of tripping on the steps of the podium, and then, after I had spoken, hearing the comment by the minister (the same portly gent that had given us a pass on the Confirmation exam). Perhaps it was a compliment? Something to the effect that it would take an eternity to unravel what I'd just said.

The psychosomatic barrage triggered by that experience drained my strength and weakened my knees as if I were standing near an abyss. The Grand Canyon comes to mind. And like PTSD, the feeling began to visit me at random times. As soon as I came out of one stupor, a day or a week later, the dread would crash over me like waves again and again. I'm convinced that these early experiences, testing my mettle, greased the adrenaline canals in my brain and laid the way for my midlife bouts of anxiety. My young mind would not countenance the terror of a panic attack, but my older mind seemed primed to oblige. Or maybe it was just family history poking its head out.

As my trepidation and hesitation became manageable, the establishment tightened its grip on my life and ordained me as a sub-deacon, the first rung on the ladder of the pecking order, and a few years later as a deacon. For a young man who had accepted his caste, both advancements eased the stress of the process and rewarded the sacrifice made thus far.

And it was during this time that I began to notice an itch that I would scratch throughout my years of ministry. That itch was my desire to climb the authoritative ladder that represented success in the eyes of the Church and, by association, of the Lord. I wrestled with this metaphorical itch. At that age, I had nobody with whom I could share these kinds of feelings. The message I did get from my leaders was confusing: "Strive to be worthy, accept responsibility, but don't let it go to your head" (head being synonymous with Satan's lair). I could not shake my desire to achieve more responsibility, more stature. I knew I could do more with a higher ministry. It was frustrating to consider what promotion meant, not only for myself but also for our local congregation. Very early on, I fanned my hope that the West Coast District would have its own Apostle. I wanted it for our district and for the men I looked up to and respected. Often, I was disappointed when our district leaders were not "honored" with a higher ministry.

There was a high concentration of ministerial power in the northeastern states, and here I include the greater area surrounding Toronto, Canada. The reasons for denying status to our district and others may have turned political as the church grew and a combination of cronyism and egotistical personalities, who preferred to keep others on short leashes, prevailed. But in its early days, the concentration of power was because immigrants from Europe settled where they disembarked on the East Coast. Members of our church who had come from Europe began proselytizing on the East Coast before moving west. The leadership thus originated on the East Coast, but as members moved west, the Apostles merely traveled instead of relocating across the continent.

During the years marked by the beginning of Michael Kraus' tenure as District Apostle, I had become a man. Much had happened during the thirteen years since his arrival. I went on my first missionary trip to Guam in Micronesia. My best friend and I, both deacons, shelled out roughly a grand each for that adventure after we'd heard a rousing pitch from Kraus, who said that the California ministers should "invade" the Pacific islands. It may have been the urgency that Kraus introduced into our lives by his keen focus on spreading the influence of the Church overseas, but I felt like time and opportunity were passing me by. It wasn't until I told myself to take a break from pursuing a potential Mrs. Raff, that the young lady who would become my wife appeared one evening before me. We were at choir practice, and I had never laid eyes on her before. I wasted no time introducing myself and realized immediately that I might have come on too strong. But her smile while she was talking to her friend was all I needed to become interested.

My father, knowing his son and watching as I pursued various young ladies, told me one day. "Don't even think of getting married until you're making five bucks an hour!" I still get a kick out of that, knowing the number I would have calculated had I given my sons similar advice.

Beth was fourteen when I met her and, after we had briefly dated, her mother thought it best if we cooled it for a while. As in, until she's eighteen... We smoldered until, on her eighteenth birthday and three days before our wedding, we went to get our marriage license.

When they ordained my younger brother John as a priest before me, my ego was bruised. Once again, I felt like I was falling behind. This was a year before I married Beth and shortly after he got married. Bested me in two categories, he did. I knew it was just ego on my part. I was happy for him and proud of him, too. After all, he had opened a new missionary field in the Black community in South Central Los Angeles. John's field of endeavor had thus opened a niche where I could serve in a promising area of growth. When they tapped me to learn Spanish, I determined to do so and to become fluent enough to preach in that language.

I got married in December 1978 to Beth when I was twenty-five years old and after "patiently" waiting for her to turn eighteen. (Well, if you believe that, I have some land for sale.) My life catapulted forward from that moment. I was a very nervous groom, barely hanging on, but I don't think I'd ever smiled so earnestly for so long as I did that day. Seven months later, Beth and I bought a home, and the same month I was ordained as a priest. We had saved every dime she'd earned as a bank teller for the down payment. We were expecting our first child by then as well. A month before our first anniversary, our first daughter was born. That tiny human immediately rearranged our entire schedule, dictating when we woke, ate, and slept. Then I became rector of the Anaheim congregation in addition to missionary work in the local Spanish-speaking community, all the while

holding down a full-time job. During the next four years, two more children would join our family.

My participation in the Spanish-speaking community had resulted in
two congregations. All of this—just in time to welcome Alex Klein into
our lives. That was in 1983. It had been five years since I had been ordained
into the priesthood. My life was moving fast, and it was exhilarating.

6
Life in the Shadows

Growing up in a cave is no joke ~ Just ask Socrates

Plato's allegory of the cave[1] resonated with me like a great bronze church bell. I first came across it during my first philosophy course when I was fifty-five years old. Its echo, a hologram of the caste I was born into, still rings true. The following synopsis is just a sketch of the actual tale, enough to understand how this allegory offered me a way to frame my experience.

Socrates sets the stage for his lesson in a cave. A group of people are sitting, in restraints, on benches. They cannot turn their heads or leave. Behind them, individuals manipulate items like puppeteers. Fires burning behind those puppeteers, project images on the walls before the prisoners' eyes. Those moving shadows represent the only reality available in the cave. The only reality they've ever known.

One prisoner escapes and makes his way toward another source of light. This leads him out of the cave and to natural light and freedom. He is now challenged to consider a new reality. Everything he once believed was true, he now knows, was contrived. His thoughts return to those still chained in ignorance. He returns to share what he has discovered, but it does not end well for him. Those he wants to set loose will not accept his story as truth. Everything they know is all around them. To protect their version of reality, they take his life.

---

1. See Appendix 1

When I first heard this story, I did not realize that this allegory would take on a greater meaning for me and encompass my entire life. At the time, I could fit the fifty-five years of my life into this scenario, and a little over a decade remained of my journey before I could claim to be the character that had escaped to a bright, new reality. But for now, I want to use the allegory to talk about my childhood and how that part of my life resembled life in that cave.

My parents had grown up living in the same cave and chained to those same benches. When it was my turn to learn about my place in the world, they told me that those shadows (ideals) comprised everything of importance in our lives. My parents did their best to help us children understand that world and point out its benefits. If we complained, "Why do we have to go to church again today?" They gave their best answers relative to their own experience.

When the time came to start my public education, I entered the school system having only one single point of view regarding life on this planet. All of my family, and the only friends we had, were citizens of that cave. Some of them, our ministers, were the ones who walked behind us in front of the fire, pulling the strings that made the shadows come to life on those walls.

Everything I had known since birth and for the first five years on this planet played out in that cave. However, when I stepped into my kindergarten class and sat with my legs crossed on the floor mat like the other kids, I did not realize that every child in that classroom had a different reality from mine.

The religious culture of the cave had followed me like a dark cloud as I stepped into the real world, and the dynamics did not change as I grew older. I've given this a lot of thought over the years. The friends and cousins I went to church with attended the same public schools as I did. Our ages, of course, separated us into different grades. My brother and sister were two and four years behind me, so we did not cross paths.

There are many factors that could have almost always made me feel alone or different from my peers. Not that I mind being alone with my own thoughts. I tend to distrust extroverts and question their enthusiasm. Which, I suppose, makes me an introvert. Some families I knew from our church seemed to adjust easier to folks on the outside than I remember being allowed to, the single difference being that their fathers were not ministers in the church. In retrospect, I understand that their parents interpreted the shadows differently than mine did. This offered their children the opportunity to make friends outside the cave. I'm not sure why I had so few friends outside the church, but I believe it was most likely a combination of shyness, my fear of being judged about my beliefs (which I may have withheld for that very reason), and a personality not prone to socializing.

As a child, I did not understand the concept of elitism. That would come years later. But I believe that early on, I sensed that judging others was counterproductive. It does not appear that it was in my nature when I was a child to question authority. We were told that we live in the world, but we should not be a part of it.

When I pestered my parents to allow me to take part in a costume parade (I believe it was a May Day parade), they finally gave in. But their reluctance to let me take part made me feel different. I wanted to fit in; they preferred that I didn't. I feared disappointing both my parents and potential friends. I wore a Rams jersey and a helmet and walked around the maypole, and I remember being so conflicted that any joy I thought the day might bring never materialized. Whatever voodoo our culture had inflicted on me robbed me as I joined the parade. To this day, I still struggle in social situations.

Because of this struggle, I adapted. And became a hermit of sorts. Afraid to engage with other children I met outside the Church, I'd merely peek out of my cave.

I remember only one friend from elementary school, a boy named Rainer. We walked to school together. I remember he had short curly hair, which reminded me of a picture of my Uncle Ray when he was a boy. Claiming him as a friend is a bit of a stretch because we spent such brief moments together walking, and I don't recall a single conversation.

The name Dicky still takes me back to those days. Dicky was a bully with a round face, a short kid with a wide build and a blond, flattop haircut. And freckles. I recall two times when we crossed paths. One time, he bullied me into stealing a Popsicle from a store on the way home from school. My gut was too twisted to enjoy such plunder. The second occasion came when I had somehow upset him to the point that he demanded I meet him at the flagpole after school. I don't recall what set him off, but it took little to light his fuse. Those were the days when meeting at a flagpole to settle disputes was the thing to do. He intended to duke it out. I lit out the back door at the sound of the bell and ran through the playground, which placed me opposite the direction that would take me home. I had just doubled back on the street furthest from the pole when he spotted me. He and his goons began chasing me.

I did have some moves though, and thinking on my feet, I decided to visit a senior couple I knew from church. I remembered visiting them at their home before with my parents. They lived just a block from my school. This would be my first official home visit as the son of a minister. With Dicky and his gang trailing half a block behind me, I ran up to their screen door which hung partially open, pounded on it, but my knuckles just bounced off, so I switched to the harder main door until it opened. The sweet couple must have sensed my urgency, might have thought I needed to pee. No matter, now I was safe. I believe I enjoyed a lemonade before I convinced them there was no need to call my folks by fabricating some yarn that I imagine they knew was contrived. With the threat from Dicky still in my mind, I finally headed home. I doubt that I realized it at the moment, but finding safety in the home of faithful members of my church was also a part of the bond that satisfied my human need for community. It never occurred to me to seek help from a teacher or administrator at my school.

The restrictions that Church leadership claimed would keep us safe from spiritual harm made me feel and act like an outsider. But outside of what? When I analyze how such admonitions caused me to shy away from making friends, I see how counterproductive that was, relative to the ubiquitous admonition that we invite guests to our church. I watched how other students and my neighbors participated in sports, listened to their reviews of the movies they'd gone to over the weekend, jealously sat on the sidelines while they participated in every activity that was considered taboo for me. I now know it was sound thinking on my part to believe that no kid at my school, or their family would have given all of that up just for a slice of Grandma's *Apfelkuchen*[2].

At times, my parents had to struggle with the same rules we children did. For example, we took a vacation in Pismo Beach, and I remember walking up to a movie theater. Mom and Dad were having an animated discussion under their breath, but then the volume increased as Dad said to Mom, "If I want to take my kids to a movie, I'll take my kids to a movie." I don't remember the movie, but I sure remember the row. I would not go into another movie house until I was in my thirties. Of course, we watched plenty of television in the privacy of our home. That makes sense

---

2. See Appendix 7 for the recipe.

because Michael Kraus, the minister that designed this "safety net," had been an avid dancer when he was young, and abstinence became part of his commitment to the new Church he'd joined in Canada. So...no dancing, no movie theaters, no participating in sports. Many of our members just ignored his dictates, but, except for that one time, my parents considered his edicts as gospel.

My dad found other ways to provide diversions, which we squeezed in here and there. And our yearly vacations were epic. After we outgrew the tiny cottage rental on the Balboa Peninsula south of Los Angeles, my Uncle Hank suggested camping at Bass Lake. A tent was still tiny, but easier on the budget. This soon grew into a multi-family affair. Uncles and aunts, cousins and close friends all pitched their tents and yelled "Elmer!" as the sun set. (I never could figure why they shouted "Elmer." I blamed it on empty beer cans.) Some of them insisted on bringing God and the Apostles with them. This was another thing that rubbed my dad the wrong way. He was on vacation, and a free Sunday was precious to him. But the die-hards prevailed and transformed our Sunday in the woods into an outdoor service complete with communion and at least fifty in attendance.

One year, Dad adapted by splitting his two weeks of vacation so that we'd have a week with just the five of us alone on the central coast of California. On one of those split vacations, my mom, I'm guessing, had engineered this neat little experience of faith into our week near Pismo Beach. I discovered it was a ruse when, as an adult, I retold the story on the occasion of my dad's retirement from the ministry.

After a dinner in Dad's honor, we gathered in the hall where some of us recalled his life. As his son, not an evangelist, it genuinely moved me to share that childhood memory which appeared in my mind's eye as many anecdotes did when speaking extemporaneously, often to my surprise.

It happened on the central coast of California, as salty and moist air, still one of my favorite perfumes, combined with the sounds of crashing waves. Dad parked our '66 VW bus on CA1, the Coast Highway, at the edge of a sandstone cliff. Down below: endless sandy adventure. As far as we could see, there lay a tangled mass of tree limbs and trunks that had washed up on the beach. Driftwood. We descended the craggy cliff, crawling across the gnarly landscape, squeezing through the crevices of wood. We walked barefoot in the tide, returning to those twisted piles of polished tree limbs again and again. Our satchels were slowly curated with treasures we could just not let lie. Then—a ruckus. My mother waving for us to come back from our foraging, her voice sounding in flashes as the wind and waves only allowed parts of her shouts to be heard. We were panting after running from several different directions to see what was going on. With her eyes wide and panicky, she announced; "Your father has lost the car keys! We need to pray."

As I shared that story with maybe two hundred well-wishers on Dad's retirement, I scanned the crowd. My parents were sitting side by side, and their curious faces amused me. And then the memory just broke open like a carton of eggs that find their way out of your grip and drop onto the floor. I realized at that moment what had transpired on that day, what they had pulled off.

I continued. "And when we finished praying, we opened our eyes, and there, in the sand, in the middle of the circle we had formed, were the keys to our car." The moment I said those words, I looked at my folks again and saw the whole thing unfolding. One of them was leaning over to set the keys on the sand, probably Mom because, well, Dad was begging God, and both of them knowing their obedient kids wouldn't dare open their eyes during a prayer. (Now, kids and readers, you know why you must close your eyes during prayer.) Barely able to continue with my tale, I wondered what the other people were thinking. I stood there dumbfounded, assuming everyone else had figured it out, too. I felt totally naked. A child in adult's clothing.

After that humiliation, which may have only existed behind my red face, I tucked that memory back in the same place where I sent all my doubts and bits of evidence that could undermine the story I was raised to believe.

While it never occurred to me to pull such shenanigans with my own kids, they still had to grow up in the house of a minister who also wished to shape their pliable hearts, fashioning them to conform to our lifelong beliefs. My parents had grown up in the same faith. Both had lost their fathers as teenagers, something I fortunately would not have to endure and could not imagine. But they both wanted the best, or better, for their own kids. The childhood that happened to me, happened to my own children with a bit more restraint.

7

In Their Footsteps

Watch where you step

Fathers have passed mantles of all kinds onto their sons over the ages. We are eager to do so when we are proud of our heritage. My father instilled in me what he deemed most valuable, which was his heritage as a servant of God, a calling he had inherited from his father.

Taught to respect the patriarchal order of the Old Testament and to form the same relationships in life, my father introduced me to men of God in the hope that I would follow in their footsteps. Mostly, I accepted his wisdom and modeled my life after his example. Whether I was a baby in his arms or a child holding his hand, he led me into a circle of towering giants. Their status as giants lasted most of my childhood. And then, as I grew up, I learned none of them were perfect. My father was at my side when I discovered this and helped me to understand that the key to dealing with a flawed vessel was to focus on the gifts that God had placed into them.

While it does not change what I want to share in this chapter, I'd like to mention this first: in 2022, after decades of debate, the Leadership of the New Apostolic Church changed their opinion about women in ministry. It is my understanding that this would apply to most countries where the Church has a presence. Women could now be ordained into any ministry in the Church. I had always felt that women would have made fine ministers, but my progressive opinions would never have found an ear during the years I was active. I was convinced that if women had been allowed to serve, Jesus would have already returned.

The patriarchal world that I grew up in, however, had zero room for such ideas. My mother and father, each assigned their place, directed my eyes to the men who went before us, leading us, ultimately, to the Chief Apostle as God's Representative on Earth. My mother had great hopes that I would advance and, ever so subtly, she kept telling me so. She could imagine me going far in the Church. In fact, I believe she saw it as part of her duty to groom me, in her own way, to rise to the greatness she perceived in these men. Each minister, defined by his position in that hierarchy, represented the religious culture I was born into.

I'd like to introduce some of them to you now. As much as my father wanted to endear these men to me, he also wanted them to accept me into their world.

Obviously, my father was the first male I looked up to, both literally and figuratively. That he was a minister added to the complex relationship that boys and men have with their fathers. An entire memoir could cover the twists and turns in the lives of most fathers and sons, for it takes a lifetime to appreciate both roles. As men, we are most fortunate if we can come to appreciate all that can be gained by surviving both experiences, as a son and as a father.

I know my dad's short time with his own father was challenging, as he lost him as a teen. What he would share with me about their relationship highlighted the most turbulent years a father and son can experience: our teen years. My father told me how his dad had exploded when he begged him to sign papers allowing him to join the armed services as the Korean conflict began. This happened while his father battled a serious and eventually fatal kidney ailment. But this is the chaotic nature of life that uniquely shapes each human being.

My father's angry response to my juvenile mischief, which was often compounded by the lies I'd conjured up, never resulted in corporal punishment. After the initial turbulence of the moment, he would summon me to have a talk. This, he told me, was how his father had brought him up. "I knew what I was in for," he always told me, "and I begged my dad to just spank me and get it over with."

Because we were ministers' kids, we were constantly being reminded that we were under closer scrutiny than the other kids at church. The most frequent admonition I recall would come when Dad was wearing his Minister's Hat, and we kids would be disturbing his peace, either at church or at home. "Children are to be seen and not heard." Or, if caught talking out of school near another adult, "Think before you speak!"

Dad was a constant anchor in my life, and once we got through our awkward years, I always accepted his imperfections, which as his son I knew well. Regardless of life's vicissitudes, he was doing what he thought was best for me. His nature was to be gentle as he heard me out. As I grew up, I was keen to study his reaction to all the men of God who entered our sphere. The older I became, the more I saw what he saw in them, elements both good and questionable.

My father took me in his arms and later by hand to greet the prominent men in our Church. This show of respect, his acknowledgment of God's Servants, was as much a part of our religious observance as were the sermons themselves. After a district service, it could take as much time to go through the receiving line and shake everybody's hands as it took for the entire service to play out. It was a ritual my parents had insisted on since we were children and as much a part of our indoctrination into the Church as Sunday School. It may have been why I insisted on applying a healthy gob of butch wax to my hair during my rebellious years. More than one minister would pat or rub my head and realize he had messed with the wrong kid.

These men, like gods themselves, seldom appeared to change, and I appreciated it when they noticed that I was growing up, even if they seemed to stay the same. That changed, of course, when I caught up with them and stood among them as a man myself. As I paid more attention to their words, bowing to the awe which many of them commanded, they often reminded me of my own heritage.

Ewald Hiby, an apostle, had been a close friend of my grandfather's. It was he who shared with my dad Alfred E. Neuman's (*Mad Magazine*) motto: "What, me worry?" This, after Dad lost his own father. A family friend, Apostle Hiby was a regular guest in my father's home, and he had also conducted my grandfather's funeral. His stern look remains a reminder to me of how religion presented itself in my younger years. A very serious business indeed. He was one apostle we would stand in line to greet after sleeping through most of the sermon. I only knew him as a boy, though there was a steady supply of these leaders as I grew up. As the saying goes, "there is nothing more constant than change." One of them liked to say that in his sermons.

I called another patriarch Uncle Carl until he passed. An evangelist, amateur magician, and expert cutler specializing in surgical scalpels, he always sported a smile when greeting us. He was the rector of my home congregation on Ruby Street in Highland Park. That building still stands and can fire the electrons in my brain, dragging out a historic *smörgåsbord* of Raff family history. My parents were married there, and at the same service my great grandparents received their fiftieth wedding anniversary blessing. My siblings and I were also baptized there, my mother holding me in her arms in the same spot where she and Dad had made their wedding vows just a year earlier. And it was there, on Uncle Carl's shoes that I hurled an overindulgent intake of ice cream during a monthly "children's service," which often included magic tricks. It was also in the pews of this childhood sanctuary that I first heard the catalyzing sermons of Alex Klein and a few years later observed the casket of my brother.

There was a *gemütlich* (laid back) atmosphere during the years Uncle Carl served our congregation. He remains an icon in my memories revolving about that church building. I can still see his proud posture, his right hand on his thigh, hand turned inward, his elbow at ninety degrees, his silver waves of hair perfectly coiffed. There he still sits, beside the altar, leaning in as others like him preach the Word.

A mustachioed gent whose oratorical skills fascinated me to no end took Uncle Carl's place and ushered in the next regime. None of us local "Highland Parkers" would call Marvin Goecks "Uncle Marvin." He went by the title Evangelist Goecks when he first arrived. A decade or two older than my dad, he overshadowed my coming of age and the early years of my own ministries. I can still hear his well-articulated words rising in volume as his middle finger drove the point home, thumping on the hardwood altar from which he belted God's Word. This gentleman's presence, along with Michael Kraus' Prussian advance on our sleepy congregation and all congregations like it, triggered years of angst in my father.

Dad did not go gently into that era. Most, if not all, of his trepidations played out at home in colorful rebuffs, which my mother agreed to disagree with him on. Eventually his home-side commentary faded in surrender to the zeitgeist blowing in from the northern invader Kraus.

Marvin Goecks had known my grandfather, having met him after the Navy put him ashore in San Diego at the end of the Second World War. My grandfather had shown him many kindnesses as he struggled to provide for his family after the war.

Just before my confirmation, Marvin Goecks, and his wife Eleanor, collected me from our home one night. I sat alone in the back seat of their shiny black sedan while they told me about the noble kindnesses of my grandfather. They recalled finding needed gifts at their front door. When we arrived at the local department store, they stood and watched as this young man—me—had his first "hands on" fitting for his first black suit. "Daddy," Eleanor said, "I like this one." Then she said to me, "You look very handsome."

Marvin Goecks would soon become our District Elder, the same ministry in the same district where my grandfather had left his mark. I thought enough of the man to be disappointed when he did not rise further in the ranks of the Church.

Marvin Goecks was the man fated to quicken the visions of Michael Kraus in the minds of the members on the West Coast. He was also our stake in the Kraus enterprise as it forged its way into the nations of the world. Newly minted ministers from India and Nigeria would visit our home accompanied by Marvin Goecks. My father would become one of Marvin's right-hand men, serving as a District Evangelist as the district grew under his care.

Michael Kraus visited Los Angeles as the top Apostle in North America. I cannot recall any personal encounters (other than his finding me wandering behind the stage as a three-year-old boy) with him that were not met with a healthy dose of wariness on my part. He was always about his Father's business and not available without previous arrangements. His demeanor corresponded to that of a conquering general who was convinced his vision and plan were an extension of God's will. Question him at your peril. His idiosyncrasies preceded him, flaring up at times and remembered as something else to avoid. I once heard him sternly chastise a young girl who had brought him hot water for his tea, interrogating her as to whether or not it had just boiled. She burst into tears and returned to the kitchen. He could not control his tone, which, in this case, was totally uncalled for, especially in the presence of an innocent young person serving him out of pure respect and love. But who knows what matters of state he was turning over in his head at the moment she had served him? When he spoke from the altar, he would take a beat, pausing after one of his clichés, searching each heart in his audience for signs of acceptance. He was steeling them with his tempered zeal to give of their time and treasure in search of the glorious promises he illustrated with his crippled English. With entrepreneurial chutzpah, he called for "absolute-obedience-of-faith". I can still hear the staccato beat of this fortissimo demand.

Erwin Wagner was the next prominent apostle in my life, another general we would queue up to greet after a sermon. Wagner, who appeared after my butch cut years, was Michael Kraus' right-hand man. With his perfect command of the English language, and a smile that came easy, his logic and wit were a welcome reprieve after a Kraus sermon. Over the years, he was the one general that impressed me the most. I came to know Michael Kraus and Erwin Wagner from a distance. My father respected and approved of Wagner and, like many, wished he would soon take over for Michael Kraus. It was Wagner that ordained me into the priesthood.

Marvin Goecks' retirement left a management gap which made orphans of us in the California District. Several district leaders were sent from as far away as Toronto and Sault Ste. Marie, Ontario to maintain the hierarchy required by Church dogma. Their presence maintained that clear line of command for all to see, lovingly referred to as bearers of blessing (more NAC-speak). District leaders connected the congregations to their Apostles, who emphasized their direct connection to Christ. A pecking order would be an accurate description.

After years of stand-ins, Erwin Wagner arranged for Alex Klein to become the next District Elder for the West Coast. He also arranged for Willie Vovak to be our next Apostle after himself. In retrospect, I can see the logic of his choice. Wagner was in the unique position to recognize how those two men, Klein and Vovak, could complement each other. They both favored the actual life of Christ, as told in the Gospel, in favor of belaboring the Dogma of the Church. It may have been Wagner's way of planting seeds for a future he expected to have greater control over. When my fiancée and I sent the Wagner's our wedding announcement, his wife responded with a nice stainless steel serving dish as a gift. It still finds regular use in our home.

Willie Vovak hailed from Detroit, Michigan. He was the only minister who had crossed my path that would have known my maternal grandfather, whom I'd never met. Vovak was also a contemporary of my mother and my wife's parents. I never felt that he had arrived with a personal agenda to correct some underlying flaw in the fabric and workings of our district or to bring his management style and thus produce a clone of his own district. It was he who ordained me as an evangelist. Services reminiscent of my childhood highlighted the short time he spent in our district. Like in the old days, when families traveled each night to follow an apostle to a different congregation each night, Apostle Vovak would travel when he could. I remember small churches packed to overflowing providing an old-time religion vibe, the emotional cocktail I had experienced as a child before I fell asleep in the pew. It was like a flashback to my childhood times when our parents would wake us, saying, "It's time to go greet our Apostle." It was sad to see Willie Vovak move on.

These men left their mark on my soul. All of them had kneeled in prayer at my side, often figuratively and sometimes literally, and pointed to the future, each expecting I would carry on in their footsteps. They all led me to believe I could fill their shoes one day, implying I should do my best to achieve success in the Lord's work, which was how they measured a man. And for most of my life, I aspired to do just that.

8

A Desire to Succeed

My first credit card is a sign from Heaven

It had been ten years since my first missionary trip to Micronesia. I was sure, at twenty-two years old, that God had summoned me when a credit card from Continental Airlines with my name on it appeared in the mail. It arrived the day after a rousing call from Michael Kraus to carry the apostles' doctrine to the Pacific Islands. I'd bitten off more than I was ordained to chew, and by that, I mean I was a deacon, and according to the guidelines deacons were not allowed to baptize souls. I assume that the leadership, not wanting to pour cold water on my enthusiasm, accommodated my zeal. Continental Airlines offered flights to Micronesia. It was not hard for me to believe that I was being sent there as part of God's Plan.

So, ten years later, and now an evangelist, I found myself on a road in rural Mexico. And I was very confused. Men were shouting at me about what may have been a dead body lying not fifteen feet from the bumper of the van I was driving. This was what I imagined Satan had in store for a missionary in the field, and it was nothing like that previous toe-dipping adventure in paradise I'd had when I was twenty-two. No, this seemed a challenge worthy of heaven.

I had been driving for hours, the humidity was stifling, and I was stressed out because of the unfamiliar conditions on the highway. We were just approaching an outdoor market. The dirt road we were on was part squish, part solid adobe. I was navigating the ruts when I watched a man just walk out into the road. The driver coming toward us could not have avoided him. I watched as his body convulsed, as it lifted, somersaulting, jiggling like a piece of meat, and coming to rest on the baked mud. All three of us stared, eyes wide. As I braked, Ron, our backseat driver, panicked. "Go! Go! Keep driving! You can't stop! You're an American!"

"What the hell, man?" I found the gas pedal and went around the broken body on the road. Ron made sure I was obeying him, insisting I did not know the potential risk of stopping to help. I'd never been so disoriented in my life. "Don't worry," Emilio said. "Shit!" I said, "oh, yeah, *mierda*!" Translating in my head was a habit, and for the last five years, the method I'd used to learn conversational Spanish.

Remembering the parable of the Good Samaritan, I might have slammed heaven's door on my foot. According to Ron, we could have all ended up incarcerated that evening. Had we stopped. *Mierda*, I thought again.

Ron, an American expat, and the Rector of the Mazatlán congregation was giving me a taste of what "our"—his and my—future, would be like. At the airport a few hours earlier, he had insisted that I drive his old Chevy van to get the "lay of the land." Its engine wedged between two bucket seats, it had no air conditioning and idled like a hot rod. That would have been cozy during a New York winter, but here in the subtropics, it conjured Dante's *Inferno*. With no time to process what I'd seen; I obeyed Ron and Emilio because two grown men were having conniptions.

I had just stepped off the plane three hours before. This was my first missionary trip in Mexico. Vacation goers stared from behind sunglasses at the dope wearing a tie and jacket as we disembarked. The blast of humidity made my body feel like it was down-shifting at high speed. Mexico was introducing me to its concept of time, and then we crossed the tarmac, a stagnant furnace that reeked of kerosene.

I was to meet two ministers at the Mazatlán Airport. They knew the plan. "They'll take care of all the arrangements while you're there," I had been told. I was expecting a hotel room. Instead, Ron tossed the keys to his junker van in my direction. Where the airport road ended at the highway, I turned right at his command and headed away from Mazatlán, injecting us into Mexico's main artery, *la carretera,* heading south to our first destination. *La carretera,* or the interstate highway, moved everything Mexico was proud of and infamous for. It ran north and south, just west of the Sierra Madre Occidental, a mountain range that quickly lifted off the beaches and fields we now traveled past.

I had just turned thirty, and I'd been in a hurry since I was a kid. In a hurry to get stuff. Mostly what my parents had. A house with a yard, a wife with a smile, children that called out, "Help me, Daddy." Oh, and to achieve status in the Church. Yeah, I wasn't supposed to think that way, but that was the invisible carrot that dangled before me. Many of us younger clergy used advancement to gauge whether our efforts were worthy of Heaven. I still don't know why this itch needed scratching or why I felt the need to contain it, but of course every corporation has a system to get the most out of their workers. Since I was a child, everything I had observed implied that higher ministry was a measure of worthiness, a reward for outstanding effort. I had been recently promoted into the evangelist ministry, which I considered a great honor. It also satisfied my need to do more for our cause.

La carretera, an undivided highway, made it clear that I was in a foreign land. It also summoned an extra shot of adrenaline. This was not a highway designed for a leisurely drive. Those who commandeered the big rigs and the luxury co*aches, chauffeurs* they called them, set the pace. The rest of us competed. This is a good analogy for the Church I grew up in, too. (A hierarchy we had yielded to and obeyed. A narrow way upon which we followed the one that went before us.) On this thoroughfare, there was always one more vehicle to get around. It seemed futile. Mexico would have nothing to do with my need for speed. Its pace was deliberate, measured.

To bring that point home, Mexico introduced us to Don Pedro, a local farmer who whipped his donkey, which pulled the cart he rode upon up and onto the highway, rocking along under a bulging stack of freshly cut tobacco. Once level and in our lane, donkey and cart delivered the man to one of the many dirt roads that framed the endless rows of tobacco along our route. Everyone's ETA was instantly reset by Don Pedro's belligerence, his bravado, and the red taillights his rig summoned. It seemed like this "breather"—a donkey's slow pace—was also part of Mexico's transportation system. Not quite a siesta. We could only bow to the ass and cart before resuming our travels, potential tragedies avoided.

Those lessons should have prepared me for the accident we'd just witnessed. After escaping what Ron assumed would be a litigious hoard of angry men, we made our way to Tuxpan. This small town offered a synopsis of my first impressions of Mexico. Many businesses there sold caskets that were stacked high on the sidewalks. I don't think I had ever seen a child size casket before. It felt like a slap in the face, death was near, ever present, a reminder of how precious each breath is. My naivety evaporated, however, as I considered what these lovely people had to face every day. I had finally finished my travels for the day, having kissed my wife goodbye earlier that same day, and it was now evening. A setting sun offering a drop of relief from the humid strait jacket hugging me.

I lay awake that night with a hell of a newsreel clicking in my head. I'd have to wait two weeks to share it with my people back home. All I had already seen was overwhelming my senses. I amused myself, watching the geckos scamper across the ceiling. The distraction allowed my eyelids to drop.

Day two would remind me why I'd come to Mexico and give me a reason to return, should I survive this trip. Once again, the oppressive humidity made mincemeat out of Ron's claim of paradise found. I let him believe he had moved from Buffalo to paradise because he was not a guy worth arguing with. After sopping up fresh yolks and spicy frijoles with warm, fresh tortillas, I took the wheel of our jalopy again, pointing us back to that rutty road. Was yesterday's victim in the hospital or the morgue? Emilio shrugged.

We passed back through the open market. This time I had time to take in the sights. My dad, once a butcher, would have gotten a kick out of the chunks of meat swaying under the open air *palapas*. A cow chewed its last bit of cud as its companion, already on a hefty hook, hung from a tree limb. You could buy any cut of beef for the same price per pound. Filet mignon or flank, *el carnicero* (the butcher) would part out the piece you pointed at.

I was both enchanted by my new assignment and reminded of the adage, "Be careful what you wish for." Alex Klein had recently entered my life. He'd already risen to mentor status, becoming a catalyst in my life that had resulted in a clarity I did not know was possible. Not long after he arrived, and per his request, the Church leadership had promoted me and several others to be evangelists. Clarity of purpose combined with the new tools he had arranged was nothing short of life changing. Together, his new evangelists formed a team. Each was given a specific assignment. Mine was to reach out and serve the Spanish-speaking souls who were a predominant community in Southern California.

Honored to be part of his team, I accepted Klein's invitation to travel to Mexico and take up where he'd left off. He would continue to travel to Mexico in his new capacity. But now I was asking myself, what had I gotten myself into?

Well, it was just a short distance this morning. I signaled to exit the unpredictable interstate, taking a resting breath as we left the *carretera* and headed to Villa Hidalgo. Now approaching the town limits, I slowed down to match the local vibe. A cowboy poked along the side of the road on his mount. Internationally known logos such as John Deere and International staked claims to trees and truck doors. Businesses bunched up closer together as we entered the main street. Shop hands loaded feed or sat idly, waiting for a breeze to change out the lingering scents. Hay, smoke, diesel, more hay, livestock, pockets of soggy stillness, unyielding. "Turn here," our guide said. I could tell Emilio was still testing my language abilities.

Gravel crackled and popped under the tires as we entered a large, open yard at Don Nato's ranch. Tucked into a welcoming stand of tall trees, we found his humble hacienda flanked by utility buildings. Between the warehouses spread a panorama of uninterrupted, monochromatic fields framed like life-sized frescoes. I would return in the coming years and note how they would change with the seasons, chaff-covered land giving way to tilled soil, seeds sprouting to fill the horizon, and then, endless hues of green fields burgeoning toward the harvest.

Don Nato's home had the busy energy of a beehive where joyful smiles and hardy handshakes drew us into their now interrupted day. There was such a bustle, so many voices, I could not make out their banter. I tried to relax. Their commands and chatter were gibberish to my unpracticed ears. I spoke deliberately, separating each *palabra* (word). "*¿Dónde está?* (where is he?) flew past my ears as "*¿donta?*" These homespun contractions tumbled around my gringo head, annihilating years of Spanish lessons and leaving me doubting my ability to navigate this world. The dizzying pace of this farmhouse was the opposite of the slower-paced culture that I would chafe at, too accustomed to city life to appreciate a simpler role. Hours later, I realized how they'd placed their words bumper to bumper, just like the traffic in Los Angeles. I'd need to listen like I drove back home.

Don Nato's bearing suggested a wisdom and a life of experience, familiar to all who knew and revered him. As patriarch, landowner, father, and grandfather, these credentials earned him the title of Don. His daughters doted on him and on us, obviously juggling their normal chores and effortlessly extending a time-honored hospitality, their kindnesses elevating steel, stone, and clay into a loving home.

Once the hive had attended to our comforts, Emilio formally introduced me. Don Nato gestured with his weathered hand. Silence came over the room. His desire was telegraphed into the kitchen, which also went silent. Hats came to rest, covering fancy belt buckles. The busy workers clutched dish towels as they squeezed into the main room and gave me their hearts. As quiet came over all; I felt my heart open. While I don't think of the Gospel of Christ in the same way today, back then it had recently become a thing of profound beauty to me. The gift of peace, of open hearts in this home elicited the message that poured out of me. I soon knew I had received more in that moment than I had given.

Each morning, we travelers would find ourselves in a new village, greeting new friends with the same purpose in mind. We always asked after sharing our message if we could return the following evening and conduct a sermon, adding, "Please invite your neighbors." The miracle of that next evening would never have happened in Los Angeles, but here in rural Mexico, we explained the phenomenon as the hunger and thirst of humble souls.

As the sun was setting, the cool of the evening drew hundreds of curious neighbors out under the stars. I often wondered just how far that mass of eyes extended. And could they even hear what I was saying?

Two months later, when I returned, we repeated the same morning-evening schedule. And again, we had the same experience. Emilio, having an extended family living in Nayarit, had opened these doors.

For thirty years I had grown up satisfied with the dogma my family and apostles had put forth. And then, after meeting Alex Klein, I began to believe that the journey up that hill was worth it, I had arrived at a magnificent overlook, a plateau. And it was nothing short of spectacular. The journey was quite long and boring. And, looking back now, it turned out this view was just a jumping off point. But the combination of meeting Klein, being chosen to join his team, and having the opportunity to work in Mexico, still remains an extraordinary moment in my life.

***

One day I wanted to share something spectacular with a friend visiting California for the first time and suggested a day trip to Yosemite National Park. It was a six-hour drive from our house. We drove through the night, arriving at Glacier Point just as the sunlight began pouring over and into the valley. Gathered near a smooth granite slope were men and women assembling hang gliders. A park ranger was checking their gear.

I have a visceral reaction to heights and watched in amazement as, one after another, these adventurers ran down that sloped monolith and soared away. It was enough for me just to be the voyeur. I'm sure my heart raced as fast as theirs. Neither my friend nor I had anticipated this bonus. I've told this story many times just to relive its rush.

Meeting Alex Klein, accepting his challenges, and experiencing the change in altitude that his lessons introduced me to was exactly what I imagined those aerial daredevils captured on that day. Viewing my faith while soaring over the valley below was so amazing, I could not wait to land and take others up to share my view and soar over it again. I wanted to deliver the same thrill to them by shifting their perspective, as mine had been shifted.

Here in Mexico, I felt like that park ranger who himself glided to the valley floor after the last of his wards took flight and then returned another day to soar with another group and share the same view in all its splendor.

I seldom came home from Mexico without the blessing of Montezuma.[1] I had taken for granted every creature-comfort in my life. The reality of how these people existed, how they made do, humbled me. Their vibrant community was impressive and a vital part of their existential success, especially when considering the shocking reality of their world. Shining through their diversity was a sameness. In the eyes of these noble people, I saw my reflection. We were the same regardless of race or economic status, although Don Nato, I'm sure, was wealthier than I was. Missionary work was demanding, but when I visited these souls, I was at ease. We visited each other's hearts and minds, no borders between us.

Back at home in Los Angeles, I juggled family life, growing a business,[2] and ministerial duties in two languages and in two countries. But the highlight of it all was the freedom Alex Klein encouraged me to exercise as I contemplated a two-thousand-year-old teaching. Beauty for ashes. That was his gift to me and in the next paragraphs and the next chapter I'll explain what I mean.

---

1. Also known as Montezuma's revenge, or the trots.

2. I had just recently become a partner at the shop where I worked, details in Chapter 12

A few years later, I would refer to what happened to me after meeting Alex Klein as a paradigm shift. It was a popular term from a self-help book called *The Seven Habits of Highly Effective People* by Stephen Covey. I found out years later it was Covey's way of presenting what he had learned as a Latter Day Saint, though in a secular format.

What I learned from Alex Klein sifted the chaff from the wheat in my life. It clarified what ought to be most important in my Christian pursuit. The familiar title, Child of God, I set aside as I chose now to be a Disciple of Christ. It was a significant distinction and flipped a switch that rerouted my life significantly.

It was the first time I looked ahead and saw room to run and a clear task to focus on in the religious context of my life. I thrived on the interest Klein took in my growth, in everyone's growth, and I learned for the first time that there was a lot more to being a Christian than simply "following the minister who went before you," a cliché that was repeated in almost every sermon by ministers who, I came to think, were stuck in low gear.

Alex Klein would lead us into verdant pastures. It was quite simple. When he shared the beatitudes with us, I imagined that Christ had come into our midst.

It didn't take long for me to tire of the old diet preached so often by the leadership. This change in me set into motion mild tremors that felt like two tectonic plates shifting, one paradigm sliding under the other. Something you get used to in California. And also, an omen.

***

It is common for all believers to admit they harbor some doubts. I do not recall how old I was when I first questioned the existence of God, though I recall that I had such thoughts stirring in my early mind. By the time I was an adult, I had an archive squirreled away in a windowless room, right down the hall from the chapel in my mind.

As excited as I was to pursue this new way before me, I still found items that fit only in that room. There was still plenty of space to hide those concerns and it would be years before those doubts would demand my undivided attention.

9

The Man, the Legend

It's time you learned to bait your own hook ~
Watch and listen

Beth and I had been to dozens of ministers' and wives' meetings since sharing our I-do's five years earlier. Highland Park was the congregation I'd grown up in. It was about thirty minutes from home, and driving there gave Beth and me uninterrupted time to talk. That was as close to a date night as we could pull off in those days. We left our two daughters with a sitter. At the time, Beth was expecting our first son, and tonight, Alex Klein would serve us for the first time since becoming the new District Leader.

There was something about the lure of the water cooler in my old stomping grounds. It still served up the same treat and took me back to the days when that water ran down my chin while I dreamed up my next shenanigan. I recall wondering if its taste had something to do with the crusty, galvanized pipe that delivered its cool relief. I still liked the taste, if for nothing more than the nostalgia. I always stopped at the water cooler first. So did others I knew back when.

That night I would sing baritone in the men's choir, which was the exclusive choir for such meetings. It was the only choir (composed entirely of ministers) I had time to sing in, thanks to my other responsibilities. The comradery and the soaring harmonies we wove together made this my happy place, and this simple role was a welcome break from the anxiety typically associated with my usual duties.

So much had changed since I was a boy sitting in those pews. All thanks to Michael Kraus, who had designed a top-down system which represented his concept of Heaven on Earth. The order of every service had a polished meter to it. The clock in the sacristy and the watch of the choir director and organist were synchronized in advance so that every minute that ticked away produced the desired effect. After our choir had serenaded the congregation with three songs and the organist had played one verse of the opening hymn, exactly one minute of silence (which amplified a cough or candy wrapper) glided by before a switch in the sacristy sent photons to flood the cross behind the altar. Next came a signal for the organists to punch it, something that always got the adrenaline going when I was an organist, especially if it was a pipe organ. The congregants stood to welcome God's messengers, who filed out and into their seats while voices belted out a hymn scored in the sixteenth century, an ancient song that would have said a great deal to an outsider about the conservative gait of our church, but for us, it was a welcome hug from the past.

And then Alex Klein stepped out before us as our *new* District Elder. It was our first chance to size up the guy from St. Louis. At least, we knew, he was going to move here and not manage from afar. The man he was replacing had often said there was nothing more constant than change. This kind of adjustment had happened before and, like a metronome, could change the pace of things to come. Would it move our organization forward a minute or would it slip and remain unchanged? No one expected a time warp.

The old song now silent, hymnals clunked, slipping back into the pews and a calm settled in before we heard the words that every minister in the NAC used to preface every opening prayer. Alex Klein, cast off from the shore of Galilee and spoke to us, "In the name of God, the Father, the Son, and the Holy Ghost."

***

Just a few weeks earlier, I had watched Klein take his place on the stage for an impromptu district service in the Glendale High School auditorium. My first impressions of the man had been mixed. The national leader of our Church had called a special service simply because he could, because he was Michael Kraus, and he had a reason for everything, which we would find out when he was good and ready. He was good and ready now. On a weeknight, not a Sunday, the usual holy day for such events, he had dropped in, probably on his way home from a missionary trip overseas. My dad, one of three district evangelists in the Los Angeles Basin, told me that a visitor from St. Louis, and also a District Evangelist, was part of the entourage. I knew every one of the ministers who were sitting adjacent to the altar. I looked more closely. Yeah, I thought, that must be him: Alex Klein. He was a sharp dresser, at least as sharp as you can be in a sea of black suits and ties, white shirts, and polished wing tips. He looked to be about a decade younger than my dad. He sat there perched like a satisfied cat on a windowsill; purring as if he held a mouse in his mouth. Did he look too smug? It was too early to tell. He appeared quite comfortable in his skin. But something was setting off alarms in me. He was observing us as we were observing him.

Worldwide, the congregations of the NAC were organized into districts at the country, state, and municipal levels. When circumstances required change, or Michael Kraus deemed it necessary in his district, he made changes.

That evening, Michael Kraus introduced Alex Klein and ordained him as our new District Elder. This eliminated the local talent, my dad included, from the list of possible candidates for that position. The mystery was revealed. Younger blood was the solution that Kraus had chosen. It turned out to be fortuitous.

Los Angeles had always been the center of the West Coast District of the Church because it had the most members. My grandfather had once held the position of District Elder in 1935 after he had transplanted his family to sunny California from icy Brooklyn. When Grandpa arrived, there were fifty-nine members living between Los Angeles and the Mexican border. Alex Klein was assuming responsibility for a district that now included six states on the West Coast, a portion of Mexico, and the Pacific Islands. I was thirty years old when I met him, the same age as Jesus when he began teaching.

***

The hymn we had just sung in anticipation of his first service, and the silence that followed, would be the last steps I took in my old skin. Something was about to happen to me and many of the folks who sat around me. It would change some of us forever.

Up to that point, everything that brought us to that silence was a part of our practiced etiquette. Every soul in attendance had experienced that moment hundreds of times. We had no reason to expect anything more than a seasoned minister plying his talents, the very talents that had brought him up in the ranks of the Church and now placed him at that altar looking out over us.

We knew virtually nothing about this new man. He had not yet moved from St. Louis and would make several trips out to his new district in preparation for his family's move. Now, waiting for his sermon, I still only had my first impression of him to go on. Everyone gathered that evening had been through this kind of unveiling before. What had Kraus sent us? A lion or a pussycat?

What still radiates in me after all the time that separates me from that original moment is a satisfyingly emotional warmth that is just as verifiable as the cosmic background radiation which provides evidence of the Big Bang. It is my point of reference and proof that this unique and articulate man named Alex Klein was the catalyst for my transformation. Something extraordinary would take hold of me over the course of the next few months and years as I came to know the Lord, and myself through Klein's perspective. And I'm not alone in considering his arrival as a transformative event.

I cannot remember the scripture he chose or the specific content of his sermon. What I can say for sure is that it was a verse from one of the four Gospels. Here are two verses that still stand out as memorable from those early weeks and months.

"And this is life eternal, that they might know thee the only true God, and Jesus Christ, whom thou hast sent" (John 17:3, KJV).

"And when his disciples James and John saw this, they said, Lord, wilt thou that we command fire to come down from heaven, and consume them, even as Elias did? But he turned and rebuked them and said, ye know not what manner of spirit ye are of." (Luke 9:54-55, KJV).

This second verse, and how Klein presented it, stopped me in my tracks. His words placed a mirror before me, and the reflection was not at all flattering. In essence, it showed me the Old Testament ways, the legalism and heavy-handedness that was prevalent in the Church I had grown up in. Michael Kraus had an Old Testament side which often seemed to call down fire on anyone not in agreement with his way of doing things. In my own way, I had emulated Kraus and backed his vision, albeit in a softer manner.

Other lessons derived from these Christ-centered events may have been the catalysts for changes in others. For me, it was that verse from Luke 9 that slapped me in the face and woke me up. Like a worker bee disconnected from the hive, I snapped out of the habit and form I had previously bowed to. My transformation began in that first service. Alex Klein considered himself primarily a teacher, not necessarily the mid-manager position his ministry implied.

A series of switches had been thrown in my mind, and from that moment, I went about my life on the freshly laid track. I remember the sensation I felt while sitting in the pew. For the first time in my life, Christ stood before me. The Apostle who had stood at the top of my pyramid, had been reordered, and rightfully so, based on my new perspective. Christ and the Gospel now held the most prominent place in my revamped world.

In the following weeks and months, I would realize just how significantly this shift had affected my life. I hoped that many of my frustrations stemming from the old paradigm might now resolve themselves. This new vista would reanimate my vision of the Church and its future potential. Maybe the Church could shed its musty sectarian shroud and actually become a place where I would be proud to invite a friend. My pursuit of a new Church order would, eventually, put me in direct conflict with superiors that held the opinion that nothing needed fixing.

It did not take long for everyone to realize that Alex Klein was unique and did not fit among the usual suspects considered for higher ministry. He was college educated with an MBA. A younger Alex, drafted after college by a major league baseball team, had turned down a chance to pitch for them. (Possibly choosing the church and ministry instead.) Now he was leaving behind a ranch where he had lived with his family and enjoyed raising quarter horses. He also operated a thriving grocery store and meat packing house in St. Louis. But these whispered details were not what set him apart in his duties as a minister in our unique Church.

What Alex Klein brought to California and to our congregations was an exciting new vision of a Church that actually resembled a mainstream Christian organization, a church that most Christians could relate to. His message was both scintillating and articulate. I came across a verse after listening to many of his sermons that lent the perfect perspective to what I was experiencing. Klein would never have used it to describe himself and I never used the following verse publicly to single him out or compare him. But in private conversations, others had noted how well it fit our observations. Mark writes how the disciples James and John responded after hearing Jesus speak: "And they were astonished at his doctrine: for he taught them as one that had authority, and not as the Scribes" (Mark 1:22 KJV). This had not been one of my go-to verses as a minister before I met Klein, but it would now become one of my personal favorites as I studied the man and his approach. I never called him Alex. I called him District Elder, and a few years later, I would call him Bishop. The point I make here about his speaking with authority is key to what it was about him and what sparked my change as a man and lover of wisdom.

Klein's authority was effective and immediate, its stark contrast disrobing "the modern-day scribes" which in this analogy are synonymous with many of the North American Apostles who emphasized style over substance. It was his apparent and intimate relationship with *Christ and the Kingdom He wanted to establish* that conveyed the man's authority, not the title of his ministry and all the brass it implied.

Up to that point in my life, I had sat through countless sermons, referred to in our unique NAC jargon as *divine services*. Someone once corrected me for using the word "sermon," which I consider as an idiosyncrasy

of the brand. I had never before experienced such a unique voice in the
Church, which I began to analyze and study with an aim to understand
my own agency as a minister. They had ordained me as a priest about
four years prior to Klein's arrival. A year after that, they had given me the
responsibility to care for the Anaheim congregation. Although some three
hundred souls were listed on the books, roughly fifty attended the Sunday
morning services.

Every minister in our Church learned the ropes by observing how other
ministers (often relatives) went about their work. Adult converts did the
same, bringing with them any transferrable skills from past experience.
None of us attended a seminary or a Bible college. We were all *home grown*.

Any reservations I may have had about Alex Klein were short-lived. I
warmed to him quickly. Later that year, when my third child, our first son,
was born, we asked him to do the honors. It was his first baptism in his new
district as our new District Elder.

It was a surprise when Klein invited me to join him and my dad to get
to know each other and explore the area where I was rector. In addition to
my responsibilities in Anaheim, I served a Spanish-speaking mission near
South-Central Los Angeles. The three of us spent most of that day together touring the Anaheim church building and driving around Orange
County so that he could get a grasp of the vastness that was metropolitan
Los Angeles. He wanted to know everything about me and my life.

He was on a fact-finding mission. I was hoping he might have been
considering the area and our congregation for his new base-of-operations.
When Klein asked, "Where should we have lunch?" I looked around and
spotted a Hooters restaurant. "How about Hooters?" I joked. "Yeah," he
chortled, "probably not a good idea for us."

One thing I confessed to him, though perhaps it was me celebrating
change, was the fact that I was pretty well fed up with the concept of ab-

solute obedience of faith. This was my way of picking at the expiration date on Michael Kraus's dynasty. Why not be totally honest? I asked myself. Klein had already won my trust.

While he did listen to me pitch him on the benefits of living in Orange County, he'd already had other offers. I pointed out the OC's geographical advantages, that it was centrally located based largely on its proximity to the Mexican border, the San Diego congregations, and two major airports. He would later settle in the San Fernando Valley, fifty miles north of Anaheim, CA.

My dad called me that evening, saying, "Alex wondered if he'd left a good impression with you." Once again, his stock rose. I was not accustomed to being asked what I thought of the future work and how I might approach it. He was approachable and interested in my ideas regarding the two congregations that I worked with. Yes, I was impressed with Alex Klein.

Over the next few months, he would meet with several ministers located in the Los Angeles Basin. Shortly after these "interviews," a group of us were called to the altar one Sunday and ordained as evangelists to assist our new mentor. It was an honor to be called, but neither Alex Klein nor I could have imagined where his influence would take me in the future. He had set my mind free to wonder, question, and analyze the new world he'd introduced us to. I would explore it to its full extent.

One Saturday night, after we were told of the morrow's events, the Apostle Willie Vovak addressed our small band. "Listen carefully," he said, "as I ordain you tomorrow." At the ordination, I kneeled with my fellow brothers, and the Apostle laid his hand on each of our foreheads, giving each of us the gifts he thought we might need in our future endeavors. Looking back, I see he was showing his hand as to my future assignment. While I never came across a scorpion or snake in over a decade of my travels in Mexico, he had equipped me to survive their venom.

Team meetings with our new mentor and my fellow evangelists were an amazing perk that gave us newbies added access to the man and his insight. We met once a month with him and our immediate superiors. He presented a clear agenda and a visionary approach to solving the perceived shortcomings of the Church. I had never been in such a meeting and had always assumed other meetings took place for the higher-ups (NAC-speak for any meeting designated as above one's paygrade). Most meetings I had attended up to that point had belabored the mundane. We might get instructions, rehash old, unpopular rules, or receive newly-hatched directives. There had been a constant flow of guidelines and rules from Michael Kraus. Alex Klein now invited us into the process. "What do you think would be the best way to increase guest attendance?" he might ask. In these meetings, we were all challenged to listen to the ideas of others. There was no preaching, but the gospel was coming alive as we considered how to literally establish the Kingdom of Christ within the congregations. My brain was being rewired for a new era.

After observing Alex Klein in action, I came to believe that he held the keys to one of the greatest challenges facing our Church. First, in my opinion, he had exposed a flaw in the dogma, specifically, the focus on the Apostolic ministry and its emphasis on rules and procedures which overshadowed the Gospel of Christ. Second, having adjusted his approach to our faith using his corrected version of the dogma, Klein presented sermons which, compared to anyone else's I had heard in my life, were extraordinary. He did not need to point this out or nail his thesis on any door. Most congregants, convinced of his skills, walked out of one of his sermons feeling as if they'd finally found a capable spiritual chiropractor. They felt like their faith was restored in the clergy and they were ready to exercise their faith. At least that was my experience, and once I had learned the technique. I, too, setup my practice, figuratively speaking.

Klein's superiors, however, did not consider his talent in the same way as those of us who were learning so much from him. If anything, Alex Klein represented a threat to their authority, which would in the future magnify many of the deterrents to growth in the Church. I would come to believe that a major obstacle to change had already been grandfathered into the organization.

10

Unequally Yoked

Scrambled or over easy? Don't make me laugh ~This is serious

I remember once, after a Sunday morning service, standing in the driveway of the Anaheim church with Earl Buehner. He was a priest, and we both served in the Anaheim congregation. The last ones to leave, we each pulled on a gate to close the parking area.

Earl, affectionately called Priest B[1], had followed Alex Klein from St. Louis. They were cousins, and I admit, I was a bit jealous that he was part of such an impressive lineage. I imagined them playing together as boys in Tom Sawyer's backyard, as it were, along the Mississippi, Alex with a slingshot in his back pocket, and Earl wondering if he was old enough to be having so much fun. Closing the gates was a rare opportunity for us to share a moment free of the busyness that normally placed us in different parts of God's Garden.

"How are things, Earl?" I asked.

---

1. His last name was pronounced Bean-er. When I told Jose Moreno, a young priest in the Lynwood Spanish speaking congregation that Priest Buehner was to be their new rector, his mouth dropped open. "You're kidding me, right?" For those not familiar with the term -beaner-, it is a derogatory term, if not the worst insult one can use to describe a MexicanAmerican person.

"Any better, I couldn't stand it." Three years had passed since Alex Klein had moved to California and Earl's answer, a cherished saying borrowed from his dad, described my level of enthusiasm perfectly.

Klein was pitching strikes, and we were knocking them out of the park. No one on our team expected the call from the head office that sent us a new manager.

***

The first time I heard Leonard Kolb's name was at the end of a Chief Apostle service that was transmitted to all congregation in the United States and Canada via a satellite link. For us on the West Coast, a live transmission of this kind often meant that we had to be at church before 7:00 a.m.

Kolb and several other ministers were asked to come to the front of the church and stand before the altar. When the choir had finished its anthem, the Chief Apostle joined those men and explained to us all which ministry each group of men would receive. It was customary that the Chief Apostle ordained all higher ministries in the Church: Bishops, Apostles, and in this instance District Apostle Helpers, a designation Michael Kraus had asked to be created to manage the growing number of apostle's being ordained in the overseas districts. This designation allowed for apostles to be placed under the care of these "helpers," who then reported to their District Apostle, another rung in the hierarchy. Michael Kraus beamed like a new father from the altar in Kitchener, Ontario, Canada, as the Chief Apostle installed more generals to assist him with his invasion plans.

Leonard Kolb Sr. was ordained as an Apostle and, along with several other existing apostles, given the designation as a District Apostle Helper.

It was quite a jump in the hierarchy to wake up as a District Elder that morning and leave the church a few hours later with his new ministry and all it implied.

We would find out further that the new Apostle would be placed in charge of several areas previously cared for by other Apostles, some of whom also had been commissioned as District Apostle Helpers that morning. The districts under Alex Klein were now placed under Leonard Kolb's direction. These men were never called District Apostle Helpers in normal conversation. The title was a managerial designation and used when necessary to establish areas of responsibility.

Like Alex Klein, we had no way of knowing who Leonard Kolb was or what to expect from him. Prior to meeting Alex Klein, I'd had only one concept of an Apostle and how to relate to his ministry. I grew up regarding these men in the same way my parents and other adults did. Mostly, they were always placed on a pedestal and revered as God's Ambassadors, a lofty designation. We were taught to look up to them, to follow their examples, and obey their instructions.

Up to that point in my life, that narrow focus on the ministry had overshadowed any kind of Christ-centered approach. But now, thanks to Alex Klein, Christ was the tip of my spear. I never imagined that I would be so adamant about my new paradigm as to need a weapon to defend it before anyone. I could not imagine that someone looking through the same lens as I did would not come to the same conclusion. It appeared to me that most, if not all, ministers in the Los Angeles area had accepted and agreed with Klein's representation of Christ as the head of the Church.

Klein's leadership style was both inviting and inclusive. His message had allowed me to refocus my beliefs, illuminating the one thing—the most important individual—missing from my concept of Christianity. This presented a clear picture to me of how an Apostle, or ambassador of Christ, ought to express and approach his agency. During Willie Vovak's time as our Apostle, which included my complete transformation under Alex Klein, I don't recall a sermon of his clashing with my new point of view in a substantive way. I wish I could report that other ministers in the North American District were as Christ-centered as Klein had been. He was the first minister I had met in my adult lifetime whose default state-of-mind was Christ-centered. For years, I would nurse the naïve expectation that he too would be called on to be an Apostle. It was a dream I could not shake.

Leonard Kolb presented himself as a friend. I could relate to him on several levels because he reminded me of my dad, easy going and *gemutlich* on the exterior. Like many members in the Church, he was of German heritage, second generation, and we both knew our way around a plate of *Spätzle* and *Rouladen*. He was also a self-made man, a hardworking carpenter who had built several related businesses into a successful enterprise. But it did not take me long to determine that behind his charming smile lay a concept of the Church doctrine that would never again resemble mine. During the two decades when our lives intersected, he acted the *mensch*. Whenever we shared time together just outside the fringe of the sacred, traveling, eating, or exchanging life's curiosities, we enjoyed each other's company. That was often enough to relieve the frustration between us in matters related to doctrine. We found common ground on most managerial issues.

But when it came to priorities of a spiritual nature, the term "unequally yoked" seems the perfect way to describe his pairing with the preeminent teacher, Alex Klein. What I was waiting to hear, what I needed to hear from my Apostle, never rose to the standards Klein had held up before us. Kolb could not speak as well as Klein did. But that was not the main problem; it was how he saw himself and the world we called Church. It was very unfortunate and often left me embarrassed for the man.

I immediately recognized Kolb's personal paradigm relative to our faith, as it had been mine until I met Alex Klein. Our once shared paradigm raised the awe we felt when in the presence of an Apostle. We saw the Church and the Apostles through specific scriptural verses, which offered proof that our living Apostles, and by association our Church, had acquired their authority from those incontrovertible truths. This made the dogma of the NAC stand out in a crowd of Christian denominations.

The "living" Apostles in North America, thanks to Michael Kraus, had adopted his sense of legalism and had taken on a determined wealth theology. Kraus had also delivered a host of other mantras and key phrases which had been branded into my young psyche. He loved using the term "branded." The *old* me had peddled the same dogma with little grasp of the Gospel, and I now considered the Gospel to be my salvation in more ways than one.

As for the *new* me, Alex Klein, without polished brass or drawn sword, had become my captain. Every time Leonard Kolb spoke, the *old* me would recoil. He was just running on my old rail. The sooner they decommissioned that train of thought, the better.

I got the sense that Leonard Kolb saw me and thought, "Here's a guy after my own heart." He could not differentiate between "our" *old* selves and seemed incapable of seeing the *new* me. He seemed blinded by outward appearances. He couldn't see past my smart black suit and tie or my own, successful business dealings. Combined with my family life, work ethic, both in the Church and my job...all these checked the boxes needed for him to consider me his kind of guy. I showed well in the lineup, but I would lose points when I attempted to impress him with the *new* me the only way I could—when he called me to assist in a sermon. My efforts to present a Christ-centered teaching, as taught by Alex Klein, seemed to bounce off Kolb's concept of ministry. I cracked a grin during one of his sermons when the story of the Emperor's New Clothes started playing on the screen in my head. It was the perfect fable for the situation and introduced some humor into my dilemma. Its meaning climaxed when Klein, smartly dressed like James Bond, delivered his thoughts, straightened his tie, and sat back down.

My vision for the Church and the success I imagined it could achieve under Klein's guidance had imprinted itself on my mind. There was no changing it. At the beginning of Kolb's tenure, this dissonance was simply an inconvenience. As a minister who cared deeply about the future of my Church, I found the juxtaposed views presented by Alex Klein and Leonard Kolb more and more incompatible. In the beginning, I held hope that if I had experienced such a fundamental change, Leonard Kolb could do so as well. I would think to myself, *if he could just see what I see, he could shine by adopting the wisdom that Klein would drop, like breadcrumbs, for all of us each time he opened his mouth.* But Kolb's sermons never convinced me he knew Christ as Klein did. He knew his job and he knew his commander, Michael Kraus. And that was the extent of it. He assumed Kraus followed the Chief Apostle, and that was enough for him. I don't know why he could not see what I did. Maybe, rather than stand shoulder to shoulder with his fellow apostles and look to Christ and the gospel as the source of all truth, he chose to accept what they passed over their shoulders to him, effectively remaining behind them and denying himself what Klein had invited me to see at his side, a view that like the most stunning sunset, took my breath away.

What I ended up with because of this conflict was another anecdote for that room in my head where I put threats to my faith. How could God have gotten it so wrong? Kolb was out of his depth relative to Klein's ability to set a table where Christ sat at the head. Klein never proposed that the apostle ministry and the commission transferred by Christ to that ministry[2] was unnecessary. He did, however, represent, by example, what I came to see as Christ's hopes for the ministry to which he had entrusted his Church.[3]

As an accomplished woodworker myself, I feel this comparison of two artisans and their approach to teaching may help you understand how I reflect on those times looking back today. One of the artisans (Kolb) wants to convince you, a journeyman seeking his expertise, that he is the real deal. He shows his tools to you, a potential student. He points out their qualities, explaining their provenance, adding he's been called to this honored vocation of woodworking. Then another artisan (Klein) invites you into his studio. He gently removes a soft cotton sheet from an object and unveils a work of fine joinery and craftsmanship. Its beautiful wood grain, which he has patiently coaxed out of the gnarly stump, now reveals itself as a priceless masterpiece. "Let me teach you how to create your own masterpiece," he says. "I'll share my tools with you.

---

2. Luke 6:13 KJV: And when it was day, he called unto him his disciples: and of them he chose twelve, whom also he named apostles; Also: Matthew 28:19 'Go therefore,' and teach all nations, baptizing them 'in the name of the Father, and of the Son, and of the Holy Ghost:

3. Matthew 28:20 Teaching them to observe all things whatsoever I have commanded you...

11

El Mero–Mero

Who's in charge, or where the peso stops

By the time Leonard Kolb had entered our lives, Alex Klein's vision of a new approach to presenting our faith had me convinced that an era of prosperity and growth was within reach. I was excited about the future including the prospect of lending a hand in creating a more Christ centered and friendly Church. Initially, I was dependent on Klein's lessons, but my relationship with him quickly developed into an interdependent collaboration. Klein continued to offer a masterclass in sermon content and delivery. This inspired me to sift the gospels for my own gems and, in the process, ask myself how I could have missed the central theme of our Christian belief system. For the first time in my life, I felt empowered.

Also, I found the perfect replacement for the concept I came up with on the stairs of my junior high school, that the dogma of One-God *demands* One-Church and *requires* total dedication. Instead, I adopted a simple question, and, yes, it was a cliché, but only in mainstream religion. And it would serve as a litmus test, if you will, as I focused on becoming a disciple of Christ. I began asking myself, *what would Jesus do?* That replaced, *what would apostle so-and-so, or any other minister on the ladder above me, do?*

Alex Klein brought the concept front and center before me, and, for a while, it served me well in my quest to know Jesus. Probably because of his frequent reference to these words from John 17:3 (KJV): And this is life eternal, that they might know thee the only true God, and Jesus Christ, whom thou hast sent.

Scriptures like this fed my soul, inviting me to ponder more than just the profound meaning behind the text, but also the person from whom it originated and how his words revealed a grand view of a Kingdom and a way of life that would ultimately reunite us with our Creator. Understanding the idea behind the Kingdom of God that Jesus had been sent to establish on earth hinged on this concept. To know Christ was not the same as knowing that Christ had commissioned his apostles to carry out his Father's plan on earth in anticipation of his return. That may have been part of the architects' calculations for structural considerations, but it had little to do with the aesthetics, functionality, and the purpose which the edifice would serve once it was built. For this, the builder needed to understand the vision of the architect and comprehend how it would benefit all people the world over. This was the basic difference between the two paradigms I was now forced to manage.

In one sermon, Leonard Kolb shared a story from a missionary trip he'd taken to Africa. He spoke of a long journey to visit a village that was accessible only by foot. In the heat of the day and with their water rationed, they came upon a river. "I did not just want to cool myself in the river," he told us. "I wanted it to quench my thirst." While this was an interesting anecdote, for me it stopped short of the point and left me feeling, well, thirsty. Klein would have quenched my thirst by connecting that analogy with a Beatitude or other meaningful passage from the New Testament.

I had heard another minister tell a similar story in a social setting. "So," he had said, "we're sitting around after dinner and our host begins telling us about this amazing bottle of scotch he's come across." A connoisseur of such ambrosia, he tells us that it was not too peaty, just a bit smoky and was probably aged in an oak barrel previously used to store sherry.

He continues sharing his expertise in such matters until he's interrupted. "Man! Are you going to go on about it or pour me a glass?"

***

I had seen with my own eyes how the Church was growing in "the overseas work," a term used to describe all the missionary activity outside of Canada and the United States. The numbers were truly impressive, and I wondered if what I was seeing in Mexico was being duplicated the world over. I did not want the growth in Mexico to get so top heavy (membership numbers unsupported by an insufficient number of qualified ministers) that it would topple under that weight.

I was now making a considerable investment in the ongoing missionary work in Mexico. It separated me from my family (and business) for two weeks every two months, or six times a year. Despite the bumps in the road that Kolb had introduced, I was determined and more inspired than I'd ever been. But I'd have to see if he agreed with my assessment regarding the lack of infrastructure. Would the sheep scatter, starve, or both without more shepherds?

I had a routine for my missionary assignments in Mexico. This included a schedule I'd worked out to accommodate my business partners' expectations. All of this was in place before Leonard Kolb became our Apostle and Mexico was added to the roster of countries he cared for.

One of the first *business* matters relative to Mexico that I brought up with him was how members and congregations were being added under outgoing Apostle John Fendt's watch. Kolb had traveled to several countries himself before becoming an Apostle, and now I felt I needed to share what I had observed with the new Apostle for Mexico, *el mero-mero* (the big boss), as the native ministers in Mexico would refer to him. Whether you were in the halls of government or visiting a flea market, if you wanted to know where the buck stopped in Mexico, you asked for *el mero-mero*.

John Fendt was the outgoing *mero-mero.* He had planned his trips after I had introduced our beliefs to potential converts, and they'd shown an interest to hear more. No one, to my knowledge, ever asked that we stay away. Fendt and the local team on the ground in Mexico would plan a trip for the sole purpose of baptizing new converts with water and the Holy Spirit, which were two of the three sacraments offered by our Church.

My good friend, Emilio, one of the locals on Fendt's advance team, described how one of these massive "Holy Sealing" services was organized (Holy Sealing and baptism with the Holy Spirit are synonymous). My time was better spent making first contact and therefore I never joined them for those visits. Emilio's description of a typical Apostle visit only applied to how that kind of service took place in a country other than the U.S. and reminded me of an old-fashioned tent-style revival, the kind I saw in the movies. The advance team for this "fiesta," Emilio said, would load up bales of beans and rice and a whole lot of *piñatas.* They used that old jalopy van I had christened on my first trip south to deliver the goods. "Come one and come all, an American Apostle is coming to visit, and there will be gifts." The *piñatas,* on some level, were warranted, and attracted kids like moths to a flame. I questioned their intended use because the *piñatas* might explain the high ratio of children to adults added to the flock on those trips, even in Mexico, a culture renowned for having large families.

Emilio also described a sacramental production line beginning with the baptism with water (one minister making three crosses on each person's forehead after dipping his finger in sanctified water). Next, the baptism with fire, or the Holy Spirit. At this station, the Apostle laid his hands on each person's forehead to "Seal" them with the Holy Spirit. Only an

Apostle could administer this sacrament in the NAC. And finally, Holy Communion (the third sacrament of the Church), where another minister dispensed the Host, a wafer of unleavened bread with three drops of grape juice that signified the body and blood of Christ. The Apostle spoke specific phrases to convey that the Sacraments were being extended in God's Triune Name. Before the recipients returned to the crowd, someone collected their names and birthdates, officially registering them as members. These statistics became the first recorded information used to define these new congregations. I imagine the *piñatas* came last, along with the beans and rice.

On my next trip, following Fendt's visit, Emilio, sporting his dimpled smile, handed me several rumpled brown paper bags. Stuffed into each of these well-worn "filing systems" were up to six hundred hand-torn slips of paper, each with a name and birthdate hastily recorded to identify a new member of the Church in Mexico. Most of these records were unreadable. I was simply stunned. I thought it might be a practical joke. It was not. Each bag bore the name of a village he and I had visited together on my last trip.

During Fendt's visit, several congregations had come into being. They had no addresses, no church buildings, and no ministers. What they each had was a brown paper bag containing the names of those who had shown up the night the gringos came to town with a bunch of *piñatas*. Most of the new "members" added were children. I was flabbergasted by the numbers, and the dodgy record keeping.

I shared this information with Leonard Kolb, the incoming *mero-mero*, and relayed my shock when I realized what I'd been handed. I think his response was genuine, too. His mouth dropped open as he stared at me. "Really?"

I had taken the bags home and attempted to record the information in an official manner. It was an impossible task. The names, hastily scrawled, were useless. But those raw numbers would have been the information sent to headquarters and attributed to the growing success of Michael Kraus and his generals.

After Kolb took over, we shifted our focus to finding buildings and ministers to take care of the new members. Ultimately, we never built a church in a village that could hold more than one hundred, even standing shoulder to shoulder, and I never met the majority of people whose names were recorded during those grand come-to-Jesus fiestas. The souls that I did meet face to face, those that did not shift their eyes away from mine when I held a service or while I listened to their needs, they were the ones I remembered and served time and time again.

On the home front, a pattern was emerging. Like the twists and turns of a roller coaster, my joy crested and fell as Leonard Kolb interrupted the steady climb toward clarity with the gravity of his old-school rhetoric. I would learn to endure the spiritual portions of Kolb's visits, biding my time until I could return to the familiar, yet respectful, dynamic I enjoyed with Alex Klein.

***

An invitation into the sacristy before a district service was considered a perk, and we evangelists were often included if there was room. Each minister used that time in a different manner, and it could be quite enjoyable at times. Leonard Kolb had a job to do; this I understood. His job was to ensure unity in the Church and in the congregations under his care. When he invited us into the sacristy before a service, that was his opportunity to work on that theme, which I believe he assumed already existed. Seen from my new point of view, however, Kolb's monologues were just a reminder of our differences. During the service, the Apostle would call on several of us to assist him in the sermon. This gave him the opportunity to size us up. Did we know our place? Did we accept his authority?

Before Christ ascended to Heaven, he authorized his disciples to carry on in his stead, or in his place. Both they and their followers, the First Christians, believed that Jesus would return during their lifetimes. The same expectation lived in the believers who, prompted by a Pentecostal movement in Scotland, established the Catholic Apostolic Church, claiming that the Holy Spirit, had called a second wave of living Apostles in the 1830's. Those called in the second sending, claimed the same authority that the original Apostles Ministry[1] received from Christ, as demonstrated in the New Testament.

NAC dogma stated that all priestly ministries in the church[2] derived their agency from the Apostles' Ministry. Therefore, every sacrament a minister offered, every sermon he delivered, was considered to have originated from the authority that Christ had vested in those he equipped to accomplish his wishes. A priest baptized (with water) in the stead of

---

1. In the following paragraphs, consider the terms Ministry and Apostles as one and the same. Whether used together or separately. The terms ministry or ministries (lower case) refers to all other priestly ministries.

2. Priestly ministries, a category of ministers (priests through bishops) which were commissioned to baptize with water and to serve Holy Communion, but not to baptize with the Holy Spirit. (Also, see Appendix 3)

that Ministry, he consecrated the Host in the stead of the Apostle. The Apostles, (both in the first Christian Church, as well as those who came out of the 1830s outpouring and its offshoot, the NAC), in addition to dispensing the first two sacraments, also baptized with the Holy Spirit in the stead of Christ. Apostles were the only ministers allowed to baptize with the Holy Spirit. This entire piece of logic, clearly laid out in the New Testament, had convinced me that the NAC was the reestablished Church of Christ on earth. Because I grew up in the church, this concept was the only paradigm I had considered in as many years.

But herein lies the rub... This premise—that the apostle was the boss. And I wouldn't have a job if he did not agree to lend me his tools, while a point of order traceable to the directives Christ gave to his disciples—had become tarnished.

How did I come to that conclusion? It wasn't a brilliant theological construct. I simply noticed the difference when I observed two ministers, one a bishop, the other, an apostle, side by side. I could not help but recognize that the bishop, Klein in this case, disappeared when he stood in Christ's stead, bringing the gospel to life as if Christ himself was there. When Kolb and many other apostles presented themselves, Christ was, at best, in the shadows. Christ was used as evidence of their standing and therefore their permission to dictate, to decide how the Church should operate and how we, the world for that matter, should consider their provenance.

When I recognized this the first time, (in those first sermons Klein shared) it was me I saw, looking back in that mirror. I was the one replacing the simple teaching of Christ with the modified version Michael Kraus offered and which he'd franchised using the ministers that followed his lead. How Klein managed to see past it and shine a light back on the path to sanity, I'm not sure. I never heard that part of the story. But ever since he'd exposed my bias, I had taken my medicine and touched my torch to his.

This bias, which highlighted the trappings of a hierarchical system and the zealotry of minions, manifested itself in the way we behaved around our superiors and in the presence of these perceived power brokers. Somehow, we saw these men as overseers having absolute authority over our lives. It is the kind of authority that prevents a soldier from questioning his orders.

Those of us who had come up in the ranks, who had been commissioned to serve, learned from our teachers how to act in the presence of a general. Alex Klein had not gotten that memo. He was never disrespectful, but he also never bowed or saluted or tripped over his tongue when speaking in the presence of a superior. Yet another point of departure from the old ways.

Often a minister assisting in a sermon would spend most of the two to five minutes allotted to him bowing and scraping. This was an awkward waste of time. He often quoted the man conducting the service, sometimes reaching back in time to some phrase or story but seldom offering original material. Apostles would do the same if they were assisting a District Apostle or the Chief Apostle. Such routines would make me cringe.

Some of us had learned from Klein during the previous three years that there was a better way to assist in a service, and a better way to conduct an entire sermon. "Better" could mean more efficient, more honest, more interesting, with less fluff, less stalling, less bullshit. Alex Klein had demonstrated this difference whenever he'd assisted Willy Vovak, the previous Apostle, and now, too, with his new "bearer of blessing" Leonard Kolb. Those of us who'd come to appreciate this fresh approach, followed Klein's lead. It was my opinion that the congregation would appreciate it, as well and as much as I had, if the assisting minister would forgo the false modesty and just say something interesting. After all, whoever had called me to assist him, most likely a higher administration brother (NAC-speak) was sitting right there and did not need, or deserve, to get his brass polished. I believed that the Holy Spirit would use me as a vessel and could make better use of my voice if I offered what He, the Spirit, had prompted in my soul without my having to genuflect in the presence of the Apostle or any higher ministry in attendance. Alex Klein, soon to be a Bishop, would support his superior's message with an example from the Gospels and, with his articulate gifts, save us all from the usual mundane fare. The way I saw it, that was the way forward. But it did not impress our new leader.

***

Beth and I traveled to Canada for a friend's wedding. We had met the bride and groom at the annual youth conference in Kitchener, Ontario, Canada. (It was the groom and I that had watched as hang gliders launched from Glacier Point in Yosemite.) The wedding was on a Sunday afternoon, and it happened to correspond with the Church's North American Thanksgiving-Day service. (Not related to "turkey-day" in the U.S.) That particular service was a big deal and one that Michael Kraus promoted with great passion. (The day focused on a special monetary offering from the members that was promoted for a month ahead of the event) He was "filthy rich" (his words, not mine) and convinced it was because of his offerings. Beth and I attended the morning service in Kitchener Central in the huge cathedral that Kraus had built, the very heart of power. An *ausweis* (ID) was required when any member travelled out of their local area. Remember, we were known as that German Church, and there were still reasons why that name clung. We presented our identification to the deacon at the door. After service, a bishop found me to return it and said in no uncertain terms that I should never travel away from my home congregation on Thanksgiving Day![3] Kraus had signed our *ausweis* and I assumed he wanted the rest of the telegram conveyed to me orally. It was one of those unspoken little things. A secret book of guidelines for the elite. Or so it seemed.

Leonard Kolb invited us evangelists and our immediate superiors to Erie, Pennsylvania, his home district and congregation. Geographically, Erie and several cities between New York and Toronto represented a bastion of Apostolic leadership, all centered around Michael Kraus.

Now, stepping back, I can appreciate what a different perspective can offer when considering this trip and others like it. At the time, I considered it a patronizing attempt to get us visitors to see how Kolb's district excelled over our West Coast operation.

My reaction to the invitations to visit Erie and the epicenter of leadership it represented was probably defensive in nature. Like that secret book of etiquette I was not privy to, I suspected that this trip to Erie might be intended to demonstrate to me and my backwoods comrades a heightened sense of decorum while in the presence of greatness.

Applying the most generous view available to me now, I can consider the matter using two comparisons. First, throughout history, the language spoken by a people was found to be purest at the center of the country where the population was the most concentrated. As one moved closer to the border of a neighboring country speaking a different language, the

---

3. We had given our "special offering" before leaving our home congregation and given an offering there in Kitchener, which was privy to us alone.

language became a hybrid because of its proximity to foreign speakers. Perhaps it was true that we in California had missed the linguistic differences which defined the level of sophistication required when in the presence of superiors.

Second, the same can be said regarding the attitude of the inhabitants of a city toward their monarch. Let's use London, where the British monarchy is omnipresent, and protocols are scrutinized zealously. The same monarch visiting another country or even a remote outpost, most likely will not be received in the same manner. A friend who moved to California from the East Coast once described it to me this way, and, yes, it was a bit tongue in cheek. Those of us from the "right coast" (I heard "righteous coast"), having visited the "left coast" (California), do notice a difference, implying one side of the country did things "differently" (I heard "better") from the other.

But for me, the issue was not dealing with the posturing of men, each displaying his own sense of humility to rehash the dogma, but the absence of the original truths which had inspired the original disciples to leave their previous lives to learn everything there was to know about Jesus Christ.

And so, when an invitation was extended to us in California to visit the "right coast" of Lake Erie, I had a feeling we were being summoned to take notes and maybe, just maybe, we would get the picture and learn to bow lower.

From the moment we arrived, the smiles offered to us were genuine and joyful and made us feel like special, honored guests. After a cruise on Lake Erie, we prepared to attend a service for the ministers and their wives that evening. Some of us were called to assist. I sensed the elevated etiquette but resisted the urge to mimic that vibe and to bow lower. (It was not much of an urge.)

I was probably too enamored with my mentor Alex Klein to bend down and just go with the flow. If given the chance, I would gladly introduce what I had learned from my teacher to see if anyone could tell the difference. Over the years, I was given a few opportunities to do just that. We were invited back several times, and on one trip, I was assigned to conduct a service in Jamestown, New York, in the company of the Bishop from Erie. He had been instructed to give the opening prayer and then turn the sermon over to me. This Bishop offered me no suggestions at any point regarding sermon content. I had no idea that was a thing, a lower-ranking minister serving while a senior observed. Was Kolb sending me a message? Was he sending that Bishop a message? It probably left me with a slightly inflated head, something I still wrestle with, but who knows? A similar situation would occur again in my life, but under different circumstances.

At the conclusion of that service in Jamestown, I had an answer to my question as several members in the reception line convinced me that they had noticed the difference. I did not consider it a compliment as much as proof that our paradigm could be an agent of change that reinvigorated souls.

Today, I think I understand what Kolb wanted me to know. That he was impressed with me. That I should be patient. That my time would come. But all of this did not explain why he could not see what I saw (as my mentor Klein saw), specifically, the need, especially for an Apostle, to infuse the teachings of Christ into the foundation of every service he conducted.

Christ himself stated that a man cannot serve two masters. He meant God and money, but his words also accurately described how I felt being pulled in two different directions by the two men I wanted to respect the most.

Back home from Erie, I now resumed my practice of treating each sermon and each interaction with souls as an opportunity to live and serve based on what I had learned. I wanted to do so with the hope that eventually that idea would permeate the whole Church.

For the next two decades, every time I sat in a sermon conducted by ministers serving as Apostles of Christ, I could not help comparing them to the new standard bearer in my life, and each time, the verse from the Gospel of Mark would flood into my conscious mind: *And they were astonished at his doctrine: for* ***he taught*** *them as one that had* ***authority****, and not* ***as the scribes*** (Mark 1:22, KJV, emphasis added). Alex Klein, by setting an example, was modeling authority based on themes found in the Sermon on the Mount, which in my opinion is the constitution of Christs' new Kingdom.

12

Shit Happens

That's life

Nineteen-ninety would rip and tear at my soul. It was the most challenging year of my life. Three decades later, that still holds true.

By 1990, I had earned the respect of my boss at my secular work and was keeping him appraised of the latest technology in our industry. Planning for his future and valuing my contribution to the business, he had offered me a partnership in 1984. That was six years after I'd met Alex Klein. I was a busy boy back then, prioritizing my life as I had been taught: God, family, business, in that order. The expectation was clear in my mind, but each area demanded equal attention. Without the secular career I'd entered, it would not be possible to meet the expenses of my family, our home, and raising four children. Add to that my commitment to the Church. Stating the obvious, I needed a healthy flow of cash to maintain our lifestyle, which included supporting the Church with our tithes and offerings. Tithing was expected, whereas offering, a true expression of faith, was over and above the base ten percent.

I was very fortunate to have found a passion for, and an opportunity in the highest paying of all the woodworking fields. I'll describe the trials of 1990 ahead, but first, some background.

I discovered my talent and love for woodworking in junior high. Then, shortly after dropping out of community college, I became an apprentice carpenter. After a failed attempt as a self-employed carpenter (or unlicensed contractor), I continued searching for a more stable niche in the woodworking field. A newspaper ad seeking a wood pattern maker caught my eye. Curious about what a wood pattern maker did (I associated pattern makers with the fashion industry), I called the phone number. "Why don't you come down to the company," the man who answered told me, "and I'll show you." I went to a large, modern, industrial building in south central Los Angeles that housed a manufacturing facility which catered to clients in many major industries. A silver-haired gentleman took me up a staircase to a storage loft above the business offices. There, I looked out over a large factory floor filled with machinery grinding and clunking away. Woodworking machines, metalworking mills, and other contraptions I'd never seen before and had no idea what they did, filled the massive floor below. I could barely hear what the gentleman was saying as we walked up the stairs.

His eyes scanned the shelves and tables. "What do you think of this?" he asked, tapping his finger on an object with a bit of dust on it. As he wiped the dust off, I stood there, awed by the amazing creation before me. Today, you may be too young to know what an IBM Selectric typewriter looks like. It's a device that's now been replaced by a computer keyboard. This particular model of typewriter had a metal body that encased the mechanisms which operated the machine. I had first learned to type on such a machine in junior high school and could type fifty words a minute at the end of that semester.

Imagine the typewriter's metal case as a flowing design of tangent surfaces and slopes with no sharp corners. The case wrapped around the sides, the back, and the front, surrounding a set of keys arranged in the common way, called QWERTY, just as a PC's keyboard is still arranged. Now picture that thin typewriter case made of hardwood, like mahogany in this instance. I had never seen such a thing in my life. Imagine any plastic or metal item in your home (i.e., your computer mouse) made from wood. I fell in love with the idea of making industrial parts out of wood, which I learned was how all products, made of plastic or cast metals, begin their life.[1]

I felt the form of this object, like the curves on a wet dolphin, and bowed before the mastery that had created it, never mind the dust. This wooden form brought new meaning to the term "industrial art." The storage room that I stood in was full of items showcasing the same art and precision.

"Yes," I told the gentleman. "This is what I want to do!" I would soon become a worker in that huge factory. Like all businesses, watching their bottom line, I was assigned to the fiberglass lay-up section on my first day. I walked past the actual wood pattern makers and wondered if I'd ever ascend to their station. Would I just remain a grunt? When the lead in that department honestly told me the odds of ever working in his department, I started making some noise. I mean I literally started making noise while machining a chunk of iron in a duplicating machine. (I had graduated to the machine shop by then.) When the shop foreman asked if there was a problem, I shared my frustration. "I came here to learn how to be a wood pattern maker," I told him. The cast-iron part I'd been machining for a permanent mold that made the scoop for an F-14 fighter jet was also art to me, but I wanted to learn how to make the wood master[2] that the

---

1. (This was before 3D printers and (CAM) computer automated man-ufacturing became mainstream.)

2. A wood master, like the typewriter case mentioned, is needed to begin the process of building permanent tooling. Permanent tooling is used to make the actual items we see in day to day life.

duplicating machine required to cut the filthy cast-iron part that I was machining.

I was told the layoff was just for the holidays, and a month later, I was beginning to get the message. I'd never be a pattern maker at that company. So, intent on finding a way to break into that trade, I hit the road. I was feeling totally dejected after visiting and hearing excuses from potential employers. I rested my arms and head on the steering wheel in my car. It was a long wait at a stop sign on a major boulevard. I was turning left, a straight shot to the freeway, when I looked up and saw a sign across the street. What the heck, I thought. What's one more stop. I've come this far. The bold letters on the tiny building I saw said Practical Pattern Shop. Two hours later, after discussing matters of faith with a kind Swedish octogenarian, I had landed a job as the newest apprentice at the Practical Pattern Shop. The company only made wood patterns. We three employees would eat lunch together the following Monday: Mr. Hoffmann (soon retiring), Andy Hazell, my future partner, and I. We smiled at each other as they learned I had never built a wood pattern in my life.

Let's jump ahead five years in my career. I was now a journeyman pattern maker, having completed the apprenticeship. I was encouraging my boss, Andy, to consider applying recent technology to better build our product. He agreed, and we started making some simple changes that brought significant results. I enjoyed attending a yearly machinery convention to monitor the latest technology because I was interested in our industry's progress related to the use of computer-assisted design and machining (the term CAD-CAM remains a key part of the manufacturing industry today).

Andy was very aware of my involvement with the Church and my responsibilities, and so he allowed me to bank my hours so that I could take two-week trips to Mexico. I'd work a fifty-hour work week and bank ten hours, which I agreed to work without overtime. Every eight weeks, then I'd have two weeks of banked hours to cover my paycheck while I was away.

Ten more years passed. Some very promising computerized technology became available. I pestered my now-partner Andy to consider the new cutting-edge technology, which I knew would replace the methods we were using. It was a bitter reality, but the future did not bide well for future wood pattern makers. Changing how we manufactured our products was a lot to take in for him and, if anything, he was in denial—old dog, new tricks. It would require a significant investment and retraining to operate the new technology. Andy was not interested.

Andy realized the day would come when he would want to retire. Our arrangement would allow me to buy him out. One day I approached him with the idea that I buy him out now "so I can go forward with my plans of modernization." He agreed if our deal would keep him on as an employee. I accepted this without hesitation. By the end of 1989, we had come to an agreement which both of our lawyers had reviewed. We signed the papers just before the new decade began.

As of January 1990, I had both a workbench and a desk with my name on it. I was the proud owner of the Practical Pattern Shop, Inc.

***

February 13, 1990.

"Hi, Dad, how's it going?"

"I don't know, Bill." There was a heavy sigh. "I just got a call from a lady in your brother John's congregation. She said she was watching the news and thinks she saw John's van in an accident on the Harbor Freeway. There was a fatality."

In those days, we did not have cell phones. My dad worked for my brother and was calling from his shop, where they manufactured stained and leaded glass windows.

"You know, Dad, there are a lot of vans that look like John's."

"Yeah, I know," he said. "I just needed to tell you what she said."

"Well, I'll see you tonight, all right? I'm sure everything will be fine."

How my dad conducted his meeting that night, I don't know, but he did it. I don't remember what the agenda was, but I remember that there was also a district women's choir practice that evening, which my wife and sister-in-law attended. After the meeting, Dad told me that John had not come back to the office or come home. That was not unusual. Not being at the meeting, however, was highly unusual.

Dad went home that night, and not long after he arrived, my sister-in-law Maria called. An officer of the Los Angeles Police Department had left a business card in the door. Maria had found it when she got home from choir practice. My mom and dad headed down to their house.

When I got home from the meeting that night, I immediately called Bishop Klein. "I think my brother was killed in a traffic accident today." Although I told him what I knew, he refused to accept such news without a definitive statement or proof, and he had not heard from my dad yet. So I hung up, and as the evening unfolded, the devastating reality required us all to accept the fact that John, our son, brother, husband, and father, was not coming home ever again.

I had hugged John for the last time on Christmas day. He was thirty-four years old. We might have been at the same meeting or two since then, but we'd just nodded at each other or missed each other, which was not uncommon. I had been putting off calling him about my business acquisition. There were so many distractions. And now our time together had ended.

A week and a half after my brother's funeral, Leonard Kolb was relying on me to travel with him to Mexico City and translate the service for him. Though I was still grieving, I agreed to keep Kolb's schedule. In our Church, there was a particular care given to souls now deceased, or "in the beyond," as we referred to them. Based on one verse in the New Testament, the Apostles in our Church had assumed a responsibility to baptize and seal the dead. *Else what shall they do which are baptized for the dead, if the dead rise not at all? Why are they then baptized for the dead?* (I Corinthians 15:29, KJV)

That service in Mexico City corresponded with one of three yearly services which the Church had set aside as services for the departed. Congregations in every nation practiced this custom on the same calendar day. According to Wikipedia, only two other denominations have similar customs: the Latter-Day Saints and the Old Apostolic Church.

At the end of these services, the Apostle would choose one or two proxies to represent the departed. He would baptize unseen souls through these proxies, first with water and then with the Holy Spirit, by laying hands on them and then serving them Holy Communion.

All NAC children of God, now deceased, were then invited to receive the sacrament of Holy Communion on these occasions in the same manner.

We were taught as children that members of the Church who had died and now "lived" in the realms of the departed were free to enter and leave all the *realms* which, combined, constituted the place all souls inhabited after death. Each distinct realm denoted the status of a soul at the time of their death. Realms could also be referred to as prisons. It was believed that this freedom of movement allowed the deceased members of our church to invite seeking souls to this service. The logic applied was this: only a living Apostle could dispense the sacraments of the Church, which was only established on earth by Christ. Ministers urged their congregations to offer prayers in support of these "lost" souls and to make them feel welcome on the following Sunday.

This aspect of our beliefs had always been hard for me to understand. I'm not sure how I saw the practice as a child, as it is not a simple concept at any age. For many years, part of the preparation for the service involved the telling and reading of many visions that members had experienced. Michael Kraus had elevated the aura surrounding this observance to the status of a supernatural carnival. The visions which he had encouraged became more detailed and explanatory of the manner and conditions of these realms. This aspect of that practice came to an abrupt end when some who boasted of their gifts went overboard.

This service in Mexico City would be challenging, not only because of my recent loss, but also because I spoke the words as the translator, inviting these souls to come to the altar on earth. My brother received a special invitation from the Apostle to receive the Host. I almost broke down when he said John's name and I repeated it in my translation. The entire trip was torture. I could not wait till it ended.

And so, I came home emotionally exhausted to a family in mourning. A few months later, we would lose my cousin, who was the same age as my brother, to AIDS, which was tearing through the gay community. My cousin became a statistic of that scourge.

The year 1990 continued to be filled with pestilence. I attempted to salvage my brother's business by moving his equipment into the building next door to my shop, a building which had been purchased recently for future expansion. It was still empty. My dad stayed on, as well as the one person who had worked for my brother. This man, whom John had trained, started producing the two product lines John had developed, a line of (leaded) designer mirrors and the leaded glass inserts that fit the Pella line of windows.

That attempt ended badly, however, when we could not help our key employee and lead artisan to overcome his drug addiction. I was forced to dismiss him. I had no choice but to close the business permanently.

A week later, the break-ins started. They continued throughout the year and eventually affected the pattern shop, too. There were calls at all hours of the night, the sheriff describing a hole ripped in the side of a wall. "We'll stay here till you get here." When the alarm sounded, I sped down the freeway, a half hour drive in the middle of the night. When I arrived, I unlocked the door for armed officers, who first cleared the premises. Then I'd slap up some plywood and two-by-fours over the hole, and head back home to have breakfast or try to sleep. We tried private, armed security, too. Andy would often wake up the elderly guards a reputable company had sent to us when he arrived in the morning.

And 1990 was not finished doling out its wrath. That year's recession affected our industry severely. Not having much choice, I had to let Andy go. It was a nasty turn of events that neither one of us could have imagined. I felt like shit. Juan, a most dependable worker and a best friend (his wife made the best burritos), was the last to go. It left me to fend for myself with thunderheads still threatening on the horizon.

Over the next five years, I squeezed evening classes into my busy schedule. I also needed to learn how to operate a CNC mill to make the products that would be designed with that software. If my business didn't survive, I'd have the skills to find a job. By the time I'd finished the courses; however, business had returned. We were in debt but still afloat, so I made plans to convert the pattern shop from conventional to fully computerized manufacturing. We invested a hundred grand in software and a CNC mill. A year later, I moved the business to an industrial building a few blocks from my home. No more drives into south central Los Angeles. And considerably less traffic. Why hadn't I done this two years earlier?

13

When It Rains, It Pours

Aftershocks ~ What? You're surprised?

I had heard that cliché many times. It's a relative term, an observation. It was near the end of that crap year, 1990, when I noticed a listlessness in myself as I pondered all aspects of my life, including the plans I had for my business. One morning while I was driving to work, I was less than half a mile from the shop when I admitted to myself that something wasn't right. I needed to get some help. Not long after that, I found myself in the office of a psychiatrist. A diagnosis of clinical depression translated into regular visits to a therapist, which became part of my routine. Plus medications.

Throughout that year, I still carried out my duties at church, locally and in Mexico. I showed up at the dinner table and smiled when smiling was appropriate. I drove to work, dealt with my customers, attended evening classes, and produced the product that put bread on our table and in the church coffers. But the chemical imbalance in my brain had converted my previous joy of life into something that was difficult to understand for me or anyone else who has not lived with clinical depression. Depression was an unwanted companion whose needy hug I could not shake. I knew there were no answers for me in the Bible or from the men I looked to for spiritual sustenance, but at the same time I found it challenging to accept the art of psychiatry, a medical discipline that could not tell me how the medications they prescribed worked their magic. I needed faith here, too. It would take over a year before I found a capable medical "translator" to help me navigate the choppy water between my disabled outlook and the M.D.'s prescription pad. No, this was a strange anomaly. Not attacking my faith, it manifested as a loss of water pressure, so to say. Something was clogging my pipes, restricting my desires, my hunger, my lust, and my appreciation for everything living.

One Saturday night in 1990, I found myself sitting in a meeting. Leonard Kolb had invited the ministers from the congregations that my dad cared for in the Los Angeles area to San Diego for an administration brothers' meeting in which he, in a manner I had never witnessed before, brutally dressed down my dad in front of us all. I don't recall what he was getting at, but it seemed to be petty bullshit. At some point, I just tuned out. It was that or walk out. I stayed for my dad.

The following Sunday morning, Kolb made it clear in the sermon that he would never seek help from a therapist. Maybe he'd noticed I was struggling, or maybe he'd asked Klein whom I shared everything with. "What's up with Raff?" That fit Kolb's need to follow the chain of command protocol in both directions. "*We* bring our troubles to the Lord," he said, "the Lord," meaning himself as the Apostle. His old-school rant hit me hard. I was in no frame of mind at the time to consider that my decision to seek help outside the Church had been what set him off against my dad. It never occurred to me that seeking medical help for my condition would trigger such a response.

Bart Johnson, who had known me since we teamed up as a duo in the youth choir (he conducted the choir and I played the organ) and who knew my situation, found me after that service sitting in my car. He knocked on my car window, bringing me out of a stupor. "You doing okay?" he asked.

I wasn't.

I don't remember greeting Kolb after that service. I imagine he packed his bags and went home. I don't know how much time passed before I saw him again, but over the next couple of months, I got the feeling that I had turned into a project for him. And as he always did, he reached into the only arsenal he possessed to target the malady that had gripped me, his boy.

Seeing it from his perspective at the time, perhaps I should have come to him for help. It was not proper that he needed to approach me other than through a sermon, and he used a very passive aggressive technique if ever there was one. But then I was following protocol by going to Klein, a privilege family members had if their father was their immediate superior. I dug an emotional trench to hide in, and Kolb, using the only method he knew and from the platform his standing in the church provided, lobbed in his best advice in the attempt to target my affliction, which in his mind was a spiritual ailment I should overcome by way of obedience and perseverance. Just the idea of his willing my depression into submission was evidence of an ignorance on his part, something else in my life I would have to endure. In one service, he stressed how simple life could be if we just obediently followed the "one who went before us." Just the cliché I needed.

After several attempts to get our team to understand his ways, Kolb brought us all back to Erie one more time. This time, it was implied, we were to just sit, watch, and listen. None of us were invited to assist in the services. I suspected that some of the sermons we had delivered while in Erie on the previous trips were still creating ripples in the fabric of Leonard Kolb's space and time.

What I needed to focus on was my mental health. My first therapist, a social worker, suggested that I enroll in an anger management group. There I learned that anger is an emotion like any other and can be beneficial when managed wisely. I also hit it off with the group's instructor, a Ph.D. named Geoff, and I asked him if he was available to take me on as his patient.

He accepted me as a patient and became that translator I spoke of earlier. Brokering deals between my psychiatrist and my do-it-yourself brain, I asked him, "Is there any data on believers who enter therapy? Am I going to lose my faith?" (This was at the heart of the Church's stigma regarding therapy. I figured I'd just get it out of the way.) I found his answer quite interesting, if not prophetic. "Well," he replied, "those that enter as believers may need religion less after therapy, and those who come with little or no faith may seek more spiritual substance in their lives, after therapy."

I decided I'd take my chances.

As I learned about my passive aggressive tendencies, I also noticed the similarities in Leonard Kolb's management style, which was also passive-aggressive. But his idea of what was good for me fell short of the demands of my new reality. I imagined him baffled by the dissonance he perceived in me and by my resistance or ignorance regarding his unmoving paradigm. Our zeal and dedication overlapped to a great degree...except for the one thing that he seemed unable to grasp, that the gospel and dogma were as different as the beer in the stein. And yet I still experienced his generosity and felt favored by him.

His favor I could appreciate, because I sensed a loving father who wanted what was best for his boy. In another attempt to disparage knowledge, and perhaps Alex Klein, who had a master's degree, he wove into a sermon the "nonsense" his own son was bringing home from the university. "Let me look at that," he said to his son while driving together. Then he took the psychology textbook, opened it and asked, "What kind of nonsense are they teaching you?" His son's psychology textbook didn't stand a chance with Kolb. He knew without knowing anything that it was a bunch of baloney.[1]

But he couldn't just sit me down and have a heart-to-heart talk, and I didn't see the need to sit down with him, either. We sang "Silent Night" from our own trenches and skirted each other's lines in the sand.

Leonard Kolb was a successful entrepreneur. His lifestyle suggested he had become quite wealthy in the construction business and related enterprises. Of all the characteristics that seemed to impress Michael Kraus, it was wealth created from nothing but determination. Based on Kraus' theory that God blessed a zealot, we should have all been "filthy rich" (his choice of adjectives). "I don't want you to be rich," he boasted. "I want you to be filthy rich."

My mother could not finish high school after her father passed. She had to find work to support her family. It was probably different for women in the 1940s, but I wondered how far Kolb had progressed in his education. There was a notion which some in his generation, my dad included, had that education was not very important. I had the same mindset and bailed out one year into community college to start a business. It remains my wife's legacy that she taught our children that their education was not over until they completed college.

By the 1990s, it was becoming clear to me that the old ways, which Kraus and Kolb represented, would not change until there was a change in leadership. And even then, there was no guarantee that whoever replaced Kraus would bring Christ and his teaching back into the Church in the same way that Alex Klein had demonstrated.

---

1. This is the gist of the message I remember – his words in quotes for dramatic emphasis.

Prior to one of Kolb's visits to our area, Alex Klein had been instructed to "school me." Kolb had spelled out what he would expect the next time he called me to assist him. Klein had never broached this subject with me before. The next weekend, when Kolb called me to assist him, I set aside my intuition and bowed in submission. So he thought....

It was a simple picture I offered and just needed a few brush strokes.

There comes a time when you just need to trust the ones before you. Do you ever get anxious in a line, at the bank for instance? You could look ahead of the guy in front of you and say, "Hey buddy, fill in the gap, stay alert." Or you can decide to trust. Trust that you will eventually get where you want to be. Just trust the guy ahead of you. He's headed in the same direction too, isn't he?

This was the gist of my sermonette given in Kolb's shadow. I knew what he wanted to hear. I could tell by his satisfied smile. "Now, was that so hard?" I imagined him asking me as I walked back to my seat.

The next time Kolb called me to serve, I let him know I knew the difference between the standard inclination to rehash the dogma of following obediently or any of the other fundamental rules I no longer considered substantive, and the need, on my part, to offer a now treasured lesson I'd learned from the teachings of Christ.

Something that I did not comprehend at the time was the distance I'd managed to put between the old me and my reformed self. The counter-culture that Klein had created and that I inhabited was my answer to the perceived problems of the Church at that time, but in reality, the Church would never become what I envisioned it could, and that took time to sink in.

✳✳✳

Recently, to help myself process what I was wrestling with during the two decades that began when I met Klein; I returned to the book *Questions and Answers concerning the New Apostolic Church* (1976 version).[2] I revisited the questions and answers used to present the NAC dogma to its members, which I had adopted as my core beliefs when a teenager. These were the same questions that, as a young priest, formed my opinion of the NAC and its apostles. Many of those questions and answers had defined my previous belief system which Klein's teaching revealed was missing a crucial keystone. I was particularly interested in the way Jesus Christ was portrayed in that book. Part Three of that testimony of beliefs is titled *Jesus Christ and His Mission*. The majority of the questions and answers provided, focus on proving Christ was the Son of God, the Savior promised in numerous prophecies in the Old Testament. Overall, it was an outline supporting Christ's calling of the apostles and the authority he'd granted them. There were two questions that stood out to me. Questions 121 and 122 referred to the Sermon on the Mount. Question 121 simply asks: "*Which was the first major sermon held by Jesus?*" Question 122 asks: "*What is the most remarkable characteristic of this first major public sermon of Jesus?*"

Answer: "*In the Sermon on the Mount Jesus was manifested as Son of God and royal law giver. For the first time He then referred to the basic difference between the old conception of faith and the true divine will. He told the people that in the sight of God **it was of little avail if they merely fulfilled the commandments according to the letter, without worrying about their meaning**. He thus severely criticized the customary manner in which*

---

2. This booklet was often called a textbook and was used as the primary lesson plan to teach the confirmation classes when I was preparing for my confirmation.

the divine laws were interpreted and obeyed. Those, however, who honestly endeavored to achieve the good pleasure of God would be saved. Finally, He taught the people how they ought to pray and gave them the most perfect of all prayers, which has become known as the Lord's Prayer" (emphasis added).

I found it very interesting that the Sermon on the Mount was given so little attention in this section dedicated to the Church's beliefs surrounding its founder, Jesus Christ. Furthermore, I found a sentence midway through this explanation that made me stop and think. Wasn't this what Alex Klein based his thesis on when we first met him, the very point that turned my life inside out? The placement of this observation reminded me of journalisms cardinal rule: don't bury the lede, which in this case, I propose was this: *"He (Jesus) told the people that in the sight of God it was of little avail if they merely fulfilled the commandments according to the letter, without worrying about their meaning.*

***

As the years passed, I continued seeing Geoff, my therapist. I remember asking a question in one of our sessions. His answer was, "You're a smart guy, figure it out yourself." Another time, he suggested I needed to find a good friend. He was weaning me off his couch. I took the hint and we spread out the sessions. But the combination of therapy and anti-depressants remained a welcome ballast as I navigated a life which pitted rational thought and matters of faith over the same choppy sea. It had not been easy for me to balance the various treatments offered for my depression. I found it difficult to decipher how the medications worked, compared to psychotherapy, which led me to look into research about newer approaches to clinical depression. Early sessions with my first psychiatrist led me to question if, as a child, I might have unknowingly been dealing with attention deficit disorder. But my report cards had not shown any evidence of this.

Side effects from the anti-depressants became just part of my life. Several decades passed as I, together with those I sought help from, managed my symptoms. One treatment which proved quite effective was cognitive-behavioral therapy (CBT). As a do-it-yourself advocate, I welcomed my part in this. For my own issues, CBT addressed how irrational thinking and thoughts contributed to my struggle. Though I was hesitant about this method at first, it helped me cut back on medications and convinced me of its efficacy. Brain chemicals are an interesting way to consider how our minds function, specifically, how they factor into matters of belief. Understanding the balance between the effects of brain chemistry, the ideas we contemplate, and how they tip the mental health scale is a challenge of modern psychiatry. It became a challenge for me, too. Tipping my scale or setting me off were two ideas, one a tether, the other a catalyst. Thinking about that did not, however, help in my struggle to maintain an even keel. As much as Alex Klein was helping to navigate my increasingly difficult spiritual path, modern medicine, particularly the therapy I received, deserves a tip of my hat.

***

Leonard Kolb was passionate about the way he understood the role of the Apostles' Ministry and his role as an apostle, which, as I stated were already the same as mine at one time. That said, over all the years as we sparred, ever so passively and aggressively, I never felt that he could relate to the teaching of Christ the way Alex Klein and many under Klein's guidance came to comprehend its depths.

On one occasion in Mazatlán, Kolb, Klein, and I were together for a weekend for what I believe may have been a youth service for the states of Nayarit, Sinaloa, and Baja California. We were on our way to breakfast in the hotel restaurant when Kolb asked what I thought of the day's "circular." He was referring to the article and Bible verse for that day's sermon. Ministers seldom referred to "their circulars" by the printed titles which in the English language version was *The Word of Life*. They were written by the Chief Apostle and other Apostles he assigned. Combined, the articles supplied the grist for a month's worth of sermons. Klein had known my feelings regarding these articles for years. Unlike the sermons he delivered, these articles lacked the substance I had become dependent on in my walk of faith, a connection to the original message found in the Gospels. Klein must have shared my disappointment with Kolb on this matter. So, when he asked me what I thought of the "Word" for that day's sermon, I said. "Can I be honest?" "Yeah, of course," he said. "I wasn't impressed," I told him. His face flushed. "Jeez..." he exhaled, "I wrote that one." We left it there. At least he was honest. None of the authors had signed their contributions, and neither of us knew how to convert that question-and-answer faux pas into a substantive conversation regarding the future.

Leonard Kolb's definitive mindset convinced me that I could never have had the same in-depth conversation with him about my vision for the Church as the conversations Klein and I had enjoyed. I was just as passive aggressive as Kolb was and didn't feel I had a choice with him. But with Alex Klein I spoke my mind, and we both benefited from the exchange. The changes Klein had already put into motion were promising and the only hope I hung onto during that time. He and I both knew that until

Michael Kraus retired, his generals, Kolb included, would continue to tow the party line. In this, we could not expect any exceptions. The reality of Leonard Kolb's fixed view of things was so predictable, so constantly expressed, that his sermons made it clear to me that there was no way around it. His opinions and what he preached were greatly influenced by how he understood his assignment as an Apostle. It was his responsibility to be the standard bearer and to repel foreign ideas. I kept hoping that he might have an epiphany, as I had, and that he would recognize the power of the Gospel over the dogma that was constantly being foisted upon us.

A hopeful replacement for Michael Kraus, his Number 1 general, Erwin Wagner, had made comments suggesting his hopes were similar to mine, to many of us. In a smaller setting, that I was not privy to, my father shared with me what he'd said. "I think Bishop Klein has a point. The Church needs to stress the Gospel more." Wagner rightfully took credit for transplanting Alex Klein to the West Coast, giving us an immeasurable gift. But statements made in private would not change the Church. I have since wondered how these stories—both mine and that of the Church—might have been different. What if, instead of Bishop, I could have addressed him as Apostle Klein? In retrospect, I believe that a direct sign from Heaven could not have made that possible, considering the zeitgeist we were up against.

Alex Klein would never become an Apostle. Even if he had, he would have been dealing with the autocracy which Kraus had established. In the end, even if, or after, Kraus had retired officially or from natural causes, any change in the Church, internationally, would have had to be taken up at that level. It was a large organization, and there were political aspects that were way above my paygrade, as they say.

14

Two Steps Backward

Enough already

Leonard Kolb seemed intent on grooming me, on snipping at my crown as if patiently dealing with the stubborn child in his barber's chair. Our passive frustration seemed mutual. I imagine he could not comprehend how someone who impressed him so much in certain ways could not adjust to the example he was offering. Perhaps Alex Klein was giving me cover.

Kolb acknowledged my investment in the Church, which I appreciated. I sacrificed considerable treasure and time—precious family time—and put the Church first in my life. My beautiful wife, Beth, was raising our four children nearly single-handedly and doing a wonderful job. Beth was an anchor in our congregations. As we were both bilingual, we often opened our home to both the Spanish and English-speaking congregations. She also sang in the choir, taught Sunday School, and played the organ expertly. I'd like to think I chose her, that I'd wooed her to be a feather in my cap, but all I really did was follow an impulse when she crossed my path.

While my contributions of time, of treasure, my dedication to the cause, were right before his eyes, what he could not see, what I was hoping he would one day see, was the man inside, who because he'd refocused his life on Christ, was a reborn man.

Therefore if any man be in Christ, he is a new creature: old things are passed away; behold, all things are become new. (2 Corinthians 5:17, KJV)

I was fairly certain that Kolb had hopes for my future as a leader in the Church. He had often invited himself into our lives and our home in what often felt like an inspection. On one occasion, he took it upon himself to walk through each room of our home. "What's this?" he asked, standing in our master bathroom and holding a vintage bottle of Jack Daniels. "I found that on a hike," I told him. "The design caught my eye. Possibly vintage?" It was a 375-milliliter flask, *empty*. That's what grabbed his attention. I found it most curious. I knew he enjoyed his scotch. The tone of his question was not curious, it was accusative. Maybe he was kidding? At one time I had considered filling it with mouthwash...

He also singled Beth and me out to accompany him, Alex Klein, and their respective wives on various occasions, where he showed us special kindnesses. I had been around enough to suspect he was kicking our tires.

Maybe fifteen years had passed since he first came into our lives, and sometimes I found myself at wits' end. My gut told me that change was getting less likely. "Hang in there," I'd be told. To rally my hopes, those I could trust with my frustrations would point out that a new international leader was soon taking over, but this became clichéd and ineffective.

Nothing was going to dissuade me regarding the need for change in the Church. In order for me to be convinced that there was hope, I needed to believe that what happened to me could catch fire and travel to every congregation the world over. When I got lost in my own negativity, when clouds darkened my outlook, I would question the efficacy of the Holy Spirit. If the Spirit of God could lead some of us into the truth, why not all of us? There were significant cracks forming in the wall of my Platonic cave, in my very soul.

Was clinging to an ideal one of my flaws? Perhaps. Had I been living in a world under Klein that was simply an anomaly? Was the Christ-centered paradigm which he presented to us unachievable? Unscalable as a solution for the New Apostolic Church, and had I fallen for it? I would find myself asking these questions from time to time and then find my way back to the dream.

This new order, which I convinced myself was attainable, was easy for me to imagine. Christ at the Right Hand of His Father, the Spirit teaching the Apostles how to live as His ambassadors, proof that they knew Him and that His Kingdom was thriving on earth. Knowing Christ had become key to my own concept of belief. This did not mean memorizing a few scriptures but understanding Christ and his mission. Mostly, it had been Leonard Kolb in his capacity as the Apostle, and his sermons, that reminded me that outside of the area that Alex Klein served, a different culture existed. In today's jargon, what Klein had created, whether or not he meant to, could be called a counterculture. While others observed the same things, I took it personally in that this Church, this secret cave, held all of my treasure, every drop of my blood and my sweat that I had invested in it over a lifetime. Not to mention my grandfather, and father, who had themselves made considerable investments. What a cost there would be if the Church were to implode because the blind were content in following the blind? The fable of the Emperor's New Clothes, after amusing me at first, now haunted me.

Acknowledging Christ as the head of His Church, a logical approach in most other churches, offered solutions to the problems that I and many others, and firstly Alex Klein, had identified as obstacles to future growth. This acknowledgement did not call for the elimination of the Apostolic ministry.

In a theocracy, citizens could not vote out an Apostle who was not fit for the job. Besides, who would dare suggest such a vote? And then there was the matter of power corrupting those men, if not morally, then certainly in a way that tempts people to manipulate the political landscape to their advantage or make outrageous claims about when Christ will come, as Johann Bischoff had when I was a boy.

Contemplation of these issues left me unsettled, but if Alex Klein had not placed my hand in Christ's, in the manner he did so, I might have remained a happy follower, still clicking along in the cogs of that cult-like organization. I'd like to think that I would have figured it out at some point, but so many believers had not. It wasn't just the lessons I had learned, but the experience of changing so radically that made me ask myself, on a much grander scale, *what else are you not seeing clearly?* This question would put my head on a swivel, as they say. Nothing was beyond suspicion. Everything needed to be weighed and examined. But I was still working inside the Platonic cave, and everything was relative to that cave.

Faced with that reality, I considered just how much effort it would take to steer the entire Church towards such monumental change. Like a cruise ship, the majority of members on board seemed perfectly content to accept the status quo, assuming they were in good hands. I was beginning to wonder if they would have noticed if the officers on board had changed their tune or the course. Most of the passengers trusted with absolute obedience of faith. They also had the luxury of being able to set aside any part of the dogma that did not fit their personal taste because, well, they were not ministers.

If Alex Klein had become an Apostle, I might have considered the matter resolved. And even though I knew it was not resolved, that might have been a good time to take a break and reload. Besides, it would have only lasted a few more years before he retired. There was no indication one man could affect the kind of change I imagined, and I would have had to decide whether to continue fighting or die trying.

I continued to study and consider the role of an Apostle in the Church, *my* Church. My idealism concerning the concept of apostolic authority became an obsession of sorts. In retrospect, it was actually a waste of time when I consider that such idealistic matters were based on myths.

In the Utopian Church I imagined; each congregation would have an Alex Klein. A charismatic, articulate Apostle. In my mind, such apostolic mega-churches would offer the perfect ambiance to foster massive growth. As a capitalist and a marketeer, I imagined a Gospel-centered Apostle supported by a semi-professional choir and orchestra in a modern arena fit for God. Mainstream Christianity had already employed the mega-church to harness the faith of thousands. Why re-invent the wheel? In fact, NAC congregations in South Africa had achieved mega-church status in their size and musical proficiency. But I had no idea where they were on the dogma versus Gospel spectrum.

When a professor, years later, related Plato's allegory of the cave to a class I was in, I would realize that my concepts of Christianity, both old and new, had evolved in such a cave.

Even with what I considered to be a genuine understanding of Christ's message, I had been applying what passed for critical thinking to a narrow piece of the Christian pie. The cave in which I practiced my specific faith, even though it had taken on substantial proportions in my mind and demanded every resource of my life to perpetuate its reality, was only a speck in the vast diaspora of religious organizations. But the smaller the cave, the easier it is to make things appear large.

In 1994, Michael Kraus finally bowed to the inevitable and retired. He was eighty-seven. Erwin Wagner, now sixty-five years old, took his place. Up to that point in my life, I had seen five Chief Apostles in the Church, but only two District Apostles in North America, and really only one during my adult life. More the statesman, Erwin Wagner's short time directing the massive district that he and Michael Kraus had amassed was predictable. The same generals were still present, the structure intact, but the new man leading the organization was at least level-headed. There would be no substantial change to reaffirm Christ as the Head of the Church.

While plans for North America were being discussed, the needs of Southern California also came up. What if we combined three congregations together and built or bought a building large enough to host a district service? I got a call from Alex Klein. He wanted to know what I felt about the idea regarding the purchase of an older church building.

When I looked ahead to the future, I looked at the success of the local congregation as key. For me, that meant placing the same friendly, well-spoken minister before that congregation every Sunday. Even better, an Apostle. (Technically, as sub-middle management, I had no right to project such lofty visions.) The result, I believed, would produce a large enough congregation to encourage further growth. In my imagined scenario, there would no longer be a need to hold district services. I had pitched the idea earlier to Alex Klein, but he had no one to pitch it to. Such an idea was going in the face of tradition, and the ball was already rolling.

The pursuit of a district church building involved renovating an old, old building, basically salvaging it. It would be a restoration project and would need a municipal parking variance and arrangements with neighbors and businesses to allow for the swell of parked cars during sermons and other Church events. The original architect of the building we were looking at and its congregation must have designed the edifice for a membership that lived within walking distance. There was a postage-stamp sized parking lot. Klein's concern about what it said about us as a church was legitimate. Was this the image we wanted to portray as a welcoming, forward-facing Church? Many of our church buildings in Europe were ultra-modern and quite appealing architecturally. But Erwin Wagner loved the old building.

He came out to give his final blessing and approve the funds, later returning for the building's dedication.

At that point in time, Klein was less than three years away from his retirement (in October 2003). I was just realizing this fact and knew that someone would need to take his place. Was this the motivation for his question? Was he asking me if I could see our dream coming true in such a building, or would it represent its demise? I'm sure I was not the only one he asked, but I would never know. As I listened to his question, I had already considered slowing down and focusing on myself and my family. My desire to be promoted in ministry had permanently lost its appeal. I was considering retreating.

In 2000, they reorganized the district and the dynasty of Michael Kraus into smaller districts. (Erwin Wagner's health was failing, and he would retire from his ministry in 2002.) Several District Apostles would share the massive empire, which was composed of seventy countries and over four million members. That's a lot of brown paper bags, each with the name of a congregation that may or may not have been successful enough to find a building or receive a minister.

They placed the United States and thirty-seven of the original seventy countries under Richard Freund, now the new District Apostle for the United States. The Chief Apostle ordained him in the newly renovated district church in Los Angeles. This was good to see, and might have been promising, but the changes just brushed the surface and were merely transitional.

I was not the only one who had given a lot of thought to the future needs of the Church. Thanks to the internet, a venue for conversation became available for like-minded souls. What was once unheard of now became possible. Issues only mentioned behind closed doors could now summon world-wide interest. The NAC Board was the first electronic platform that hosted a robust discussion on many controversial Church topics. While there were more spectators than debaters, we were all curious as to where it might lead. Other than some self-imposed decorum, interested parties could discuss anything in the many threads populating the boards. Should there be female ministers? What would that look like? Why did other denominations share the financial status of their organization, but ours did not? One of my favorites was about "NAC-speak" words that were used in sermons and communications that did not transfer to mainstream Christian vocabulary. (These included words like *first-fruits, overcomers, bearer of blessing*.) The topics, or threads, covered every aspect of congregational business and often criticized leadership. The discussions often became heated. Old-timers accused young "know-it-alls" of disrespect. Richard Freund, the new District Apostle, warned ministers not to get involved and banned them from responding on behalf of the Church. He was obviously getting reports about the criticism being expressed. The pen—or at least the keyboard—seemed mightier than the sword. Kraus had brutally handled detractors, often directly from the altar.

Freund appeared to be approachable, which seemed to have lanced a metaphorical boil that had been festering for decades. Considered malcontents, regardless of their motivations, these pioneers whipped their modern Conestogas (keyboards) toward a future Church that was in step with mainstream Christianity, whatever that was understood to represent. Some did not hide their identities online and doubled down by calling on the new District Apostle to address their concerns. I admired their bravery and, even more, their hope for the future. Some of them had already left the Church and shared ugly wounds, something the leadership would have preferred to keep under wraps. Most of the dissenters just wanted to see the Church change. They had a genuine desire to see their congregations prosper. I applauded their chutzpah.

Part Two

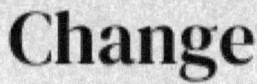

Change

15

Righteous Indignation

In the event of a loss of pressure, save yourself first

In October of 1999, Beth and I traveled to Copenhagen where we met our oldest daughter who was studying abroad and about to start her fall break. We had prepared a challenging, twenty-one-day itinerary that would take us to several countries and into the homes of family and friends across Europe. I had always wanted to visit the Chapel of the Apostles[1] in Albury, Surrey, England, so we planned to do so on our way home. After a lovely train ride from London through drizzle and the fall-hued countryside, we found our way onto the pastoral grounds of this rolling estate. Sheep grazed, dotting the landscape in front of the historical landmark. It was so serene, and for a brief moment the historical significance of that place held me in its arms. I needed that metaphorical hug before I returned to the spiritual challenges awaiting me back home.

A time of dynamic change for all the characters who had traveled with me to this point was unfolding. Still on the same river that defined my religious life, I had let go of my paddle and was now carelessly adrift, the currents be damned. I had no strength or desire to continue navigating the

---

1. The apostles called in the 1830s, who formed the Catholic Apostolic Church, which provided the catalyst to form the NAC, met here to create a plan based on the Holy Spirit's instruction to prepare mankind for the imminent return of Christ.

waters which had defined my life since birth. This was my state of mind while I continued to hope and serve. Most people who knew me were oblivious to my struggle.

The first time I let my thoughts return to this period of my journey, I was expecting to be writing about a decade of events. It would take only four years to shoot the rapids that delivered me over the waterfall and into another tributary altogether. Each of those four years reminded me of the stifling childhood fevers that had left me in a semi-delirious, altered reality, their numbing effects making my body feel ten times heavier than its usual self.

A solution to my dilemma seemed a long way off. Ministry, lifelong doubts, and vows meant to last for eternity all weighed down on me. I wanted to run again, feel alive, but could barely hobble on. Out of that turmoil, however, a solution would present itself, and I would find the strength to unburden myself. It was the best decision I'd ever make. I don't recall having a single concern about who might replace Alex Klein after he retired only a little over three years away, a very short time for those planning the immediate and upcoming needs of the Church.

After Canada and America became separate districts, Leslie Latorcai, the new District Apostle from Canada, visited Los Angeles. I had first met this man thirty years earlier, when all the youth groups from Canada and the United States had traveled to Toronto for the Day of the Youth. We had always looked forward to these large gatherings, for nothing reaffirms faith and loyalty to a cause more than a gathering of two thousand like-minded teenagers. This yearly event had gotten its start one Sunday when Michael Kraus had invited the youth groups from Canada and the United States who lived within driving distance of Kitchener, Ontario, Canada, for a youth service and luncheon. The event was such a success that Kraus invited those groups back the next year. When young people from youth groups throughout North America heard of this gathering of like-minded teenagers, the urge to join in took over from there. Small groups of youths from districts too far to make the day trip rented vans and drove cross-country on their own dimes.

What started out as an excellent field in which to seek love and cross-pollinate among fellow believers, Kraus turned into a North American festival which he expanded into a "come one, come all" invitation to all the North American Youth groups. The Church paid half our fares to charter a bus or buy airfare, and then the groups had bake sales and all manner of fundraisers to come up with the remaining half. We were billeted in members' homes and bussed to the event on Sunday morning. Once we arrived, all of our needs were met without cost. You could ask any youth group member who traveled there about Isaac and Rebekah Lane,[2] and they might tell you they met the love of their life or walked hand in hand there, as Beth and I did. We met Latorcai at a picnic when the West Coast groups were billeted in and around Toronto. Priest Latorcai was their district youth leader. Now the man oversaw the Church in Canada.

In the sacristy before the service, he casually slipped into his monologue, a sermonette for those invited into the sacristy on such occasions. "Brothers," he began, "haven't we all thought about quitting, leaving our ministries?" Leslie Latorcai had hit the nail on the head. It was as if he had read my mind. I'd heard the idea mentioned on occasion and watched as my dad had gone through times, I'm sure, that had made him consider

---

2. One of the apostles referred to the main thoroughfare in Bingeman Park, where we were served lunch, as Isaac and Rebekah Lane, a reference to the biblical Isaac and Rebekah, indicating its popularity with the couples in attendance.

the option. I had screamed "I quit" in my own head too many times, so I was sure it was something everyone at the table could relate to. Of course, as soon as those marbles hit and scattered on the table, Latorcai began building the case as to why we ought to continue and endure till the end. My guess is that someone had tipped him off, based on their concern for a brother in need. The friendships we'd made on those youth trips had lasted a lifetime.

***

Boise, Idaho, was one congregation I cared for as an evangelist. My brother-in-law was the rector in Boise, which was part of my father's district before he retired, and my parents and several uncles and aunts had all retired there, too. Now I was given the honor. It was a perk we all enjoyed. I would discuss my predicament with one of my favorite uncles the next time I visited. I was ready to leave, if not the Church, then my ministry, for sure.

My go-to confidant for such conversations, especially when my rope had no room left for knots, was my Uncle Ray. He had a gentle disposition and a welcoming smile and reminded me of Yoda as he plied his wisdom. So when I was in Boise, I planned to have a chat with him. After he listened sympathetically as I laid out my frustrations and probable solutions, he suggested I step back and take a wider view. He paused and waited, looking at me as I mentally traveled to the suggested vantage point. He next suggested that I set my sights a little further ahead. I knew what was next as he pointed to the promise of new leadership at the global level. Maybe, he opined, that would give me hope. It was Uncle Ray who heard it from me first. His counsel, to hang tough, fell on a dejected soul.

The Chief Apostles, the international heads of the Church of my era, had all retired, and most had named their successors ahead of time. I only knew them from a distance and only as much as it is possible from the content of translated sermons and articles. I spoke to only one of them in the course of my lifetime. Chief Apostle Richard Fehr smiled as Leonard Kolb introduced me to him. Tasked to present Fehr with a custom-engraved silver coin, compliments of the attorney hired to handle the business affairs for the Church in Mexico, I shook his hand, shared the attorney's sentiments, and walked away with the regifted token in my own hand.

Every month, the Chief Apostle released articles in publications meant for worldwide distribution. The "Circular" used by ministers to prepare their sermons, as I mentioned previously, was titled *The Word of Life*. A magazine for all members was known in my day as *Our Family*. When technology made it possible to broadcast services across the continents, we heard Fehr serve once or twice a year, again translated from German, as all the Chief Apostles in my lifetime hailed from Germany and Switzerland. There was always the temptation to hope in their power regarding grandiose future change. The reality, however, was that Chief Apostles had many egos and opinions to manage and had to choose their projects, as most presidents do, based on the political climate. District Apostles had broad discretion over their territories, as broad as the personalities and idiosyncrasies assigned to them by God at birth.

Richard Freund, our newest District Apostle, who demonstrated a calm disposition and presented clearly stated opinions as he served us, did not come close to the model Alex Klein had shared with us. But how could he? He did not know Klein as we did, and, as all superiors in the church had proved, their bias was set in stone, born out of a centuries-old paradigm which took hold when those first apostles of the Scottish outpouring formulated their opinions about the new church and their apostolic roles in it.

I was a regular observer on the NAC board, i.e., the electronic board mentioned before, whose contributors were not holding back their opinions on varied subjects. When I had something to say, I remained anonymous. I thought the changes being made, while overdue, were just superficial.

Yes, I had a clear mental picture of what it would take to restore my hope for the Church going forward. It was simple to put into words: *The leaders of the Church, as represented by the chief, district, and local apostles, who claimed to be ambassadors of Christ would need to demonstrate that they knew their sender, Jesus Christ, as had Alex Klein.* Only then would I consider a brighter future possible.

That said, change which was that broad and earth shaking would not happen with an edict. It would happen organically, in the same way that I had experienced it. It would also have to originate out of the only ministries recognized by the membership as ambassadors in Christ's stead. Each soul would need to experience its own epiphany after having been introduced to Christ as I had been. Perhaps a catalyst would have helped? I would learn of an apostle (only one) who, behind closed doors and at the highest level, in Europe, had been poking the bear, so to speak. He was presenting the same paradigm that Alex Klein had introduced to his fellow apostles, including the Chief Apostle.

I expected nothing to come from my comments on the NAC board, but it helped me to verify I was not the only one disappointed with the status quo. This board was one of the few places I found like-minded folk. Several of the ministers' wives, for example, were quite articulate and not shy about making themselves and their concerns known. One particular set of contributors I actually felt sorry for were people who had left the

Church and were just acting out their pain, outright anger, and/or disgust. I did not want to end up in their shoes.

I began weighing my options. I was at a crossroads and needed a respite. Maybe easing off the accelerator would help. I skipped a couple of trips to Mexico. When called on the carpet over this unsanctioned pause, I said matter-of-factly that it was time to find someone else to take over my responsibilities there. Some time passed, and then I was asked to suggest a replacement. But I was not asked why I'd come to this conclusion. I continued my visits to Mexico but reduced their frequency. Another option, one I had control over, was to passively indicate I no longer had any interest in future advancement in the Church. I would simply do the minimum, keep my head down, and see if I could find a way through my doldrums.

Leonard Kolb Sr. called me with instructions to go to Mexico City. I was to inform the District Evangelist in that congregation, whose ministry was senior to mine, that he was to allow me to conduct the entire service. (This seemed random, with no explanation offered.) Unilaterally, I decided the district evangelist should open and close the service and turn over the sermon portion entirely to me. I had gotten the idea from Kolb, who had used the same protocol when he sent me as an evangelist to conduct a service in Jamestown, New York, in the presence of the then bishop from Erie. When Kolb called me the following week, he stated that he'd heard I had deviated from his instructions, but he did not ask me why. My response was a shrug. I don't recall how exactly I put it into words.

The sermons I conducted at home in the Los Angeles district brought me to congregations as far north as Oxnard and as far east as Las Vegas. Alex Klein surprised me when he informed me that the congregations across the border in Tijuana and Ensenada, Baja, California, were now under my care. That's all I was told. I had no idea why or how to proceed and I was never brought there and introduced in that capacity.

It was confusing. Perhaps it was a test. I set out to fail any such test, especially if it could mean a higher ministry for me in the future. I was intent on spoiling any intentions, which may or may not have been in their plan. Convinced that the leadership of the Church was too far gone, I was already packing my bag. Even if I had been told specifically that I was being considered for higher ministry, I was too far gone. I assumed my message was getting through because nobody sat down with me and said, "Hey, Bill, what's up?"

For many years, I had been assuming the privileges which Alex Klein, as a bishop, had been granted regarding the content of his sermons. (He built them from scratch using only the provided scripture from *The Word of Life*.) My use of that same approach evolved as I struggled to find material and began building my own Christ-centered sermons. The nervous teenager learning to preach in front of his peers was long past his trepidations and had tapped into the same reservoir of wisdom that Klein had led me to.

At the same time, I was asking myself questions regarding the efficacy of the Holy Spirit and what influence, if any, it had in the Church or over the Apostles' Ministry. That room in my mind was filling with doubts. I visited it so often that I decided to just leave the door open. Most of my doubts, then, were a product of the struggle I was waging with two sets of ideals. Someday, that material would assemble itself before me and serve me in another way.

***

In September 2002, Richard Freund called together all the ministers whose designation as rector of a specific congregation gave them each a vote in legal matters regarding the Church in the United States. The gathering would take place in Chicago and was the second Synod I attended over the last two decades. A majority vote was required to change any statute in the constitution. Such gatherings were infrequent, only called for at times of significant change. Otherwise, the legal organization, which was incorporated in Chicago, operated behind the scenes.

Alex Klein told me that Leonard Kolb was concerned that some ministers in California would not support the District Apostle's requested changes. This was strange because I don't remember ever having seen or read the organization's constitution, nor did I know what the changes were or how they would affect the Church in the future. Nor do I recall receiving a letter explaining what changes were being voted on. I heard a rumor after the fact that Freund was asking for the power to make unilateral decisions regarding the assets of the national organization. Evidently, there were other meetings that weekend that were settling the legal and financial matters having to do with the division of the previous larger district encompassing Canada and the United States. But all this was way above my paygrade.

It's possible that topics regarding legal and financial matters of the Church had shown up on the NAC board and that was where the concerns were generated from. I seldom paid any attention to the threads pursuing those kinds of inquiries. The agenda of the Synod would also be leaked on that platform, possibly because Freund had specified to all in attendance that it was not to be divulged to anyone not invited to those meetings.

Our new District Apostle, Richard Freund, addressed those gathered. The morning session presented the business portion of the agenda, concluding with the vote. After lunch, we returned to hear the "spiritual" part of his agenda. Although it was prefaced with a scripture verse, what followed offered my soul nothing of value. It covered a long list of items, some related to the order of services: what to say, how to say it. Instead of saying Holy Ghost, for example, say Holy Spirit. Freund also addressed the use of certain funds, limits, and allowances. No doubt I had been spoiled by the spiritual content I had become accustomed to. Most likely, I misinterpreted what was meant by the term "spiritual" portion. Freund, most likely, had meant it to address matters dealing with the non-legal side of operations, which contrasted with the constitutional and legal matters discussed before lunch. I suppose that, on some level, I was hoping for answers to deal with my spiraling faith in the Church. These words from Matthew 11:28 (KJV) are what come to mind:

Come unto me, all ye that labour and are heavy laden, and I will give you rest.

But what *I* experienced that weekend was the last straw. An insignificant, run-of-the-mill nationwide meeting of ministers so ordered by the business needs of the organization at a particular point in time was actually a "cave-in" event in my Platonic cave that forced me toward a natural source of light I knew existed. Or perhaps it just happened to coincide with my final conclusion that the Apostles' Ministry as a whole, which the Church held high for all to see, resembled my favorite emperor preening around in his new clothes.

By the end of that part of the meeting, when I was hurting and very distraught, I spotted Alex Klein and grabbed his elbow. But it would have to wait, he told me, as he was rushing into a closed session. I went to my hotel room and wept. I doubt I went to dinner that evening. The remainder of that day and the service the next morning are still a blur. I only recall wanting to get home. I was devastated, left gutted and gasping for hope. The last thing I remember about that weekend was sharing my condolences with Leslie Latorcai. He was returning to Canada for the funeral of his predecessor, Erwin Wagner.

***

The following year, in May 2003, Leonard Kolb retired. The Chief Apostle had scheduled a service in San Francisco, at which time he would thank Kolb and wish him well. His son, Apostle Leonard Kolb Jr., would take over his duties on the West Coast. I ignored my invitation to the event because I had no energy left to spend on such festivities. I had not wanted to offend Kolb, but he made it clear to me that I had done so. It was the first time he had ever communicated to me so succinctly about our interactions.

Alex Klein announced his retirement next. It would take place in October of the same year, 2003. He gathered all the ministers one evening, one of the last times he would address us, and as he spoke used as an analogy, those that agree to work for certain corporations. "There is a standard that is expected in these organizations," he said. "You know that going in, you agree to that going in. If you're hired at IBM, expect to wear a dark blue suit, white shirt and tie, and highly polished wingtip shoes." His tone was from another era. He had never commented on the trappings of the ministry in this manner.

Christ had left the building.

Klein continued, sharing his intention to visit all the congregations before he retired. He would share some parting thoughts with those congregations, renewing their focus on the importance of the Apostles' Ministry. I do not recall his exact words, but he went into some detail on his vision and what he hoped the results would be. I raised my hand to question his premise, but the only thing I can remember, the only words I still possess, are not mine, but his: "Evangelist," he said to me, "I could not disagree with you more!" I stood there, utterly speechless.

Five months later, Alex Klein stood in the still newly renovated district church in front of Richard Freund, who explained that he had offered the Bishop an opportunity to stay on.

As far as Klein's intention to have a talk with the membership before retiring (some of us referred to this as his attempt to put the toothpaste back in the tube), I never sat in on such a talk. I do not know if he brought it to other congregations. I heard no more of it. Regardless, it was a tearful farewell, as I owed him a great deal. The few times I saw him after his retirement were brief. He'd ask about my dad, who was losing his battle with Alzheimer's.

An era had ended.

My ears had perked up when the leadership notified us that any minister who had served a minimum of twenty-five years in office could retire, honorably, should he choose to. I never was sure what motivated this change in policy. It could have been a further relaxing of the rules or maybe it was designed to rid the Church of an "element" which was becoming more vocal and impatient for change. I don't know if ministers like me were the intended beneficiaries of this offer, but it made it onto my list of options.

California and the Los Angeles district were now under the leadership of Bart Johnson, who requested a sit-down with me after someone had complained about a comment I'd made in a sermon. Our chat was a rude awakening for me, for it was about time someone noticed I was struggling, and I was glad it was Bart that finally let me unburden myself. I had known Bart for many years. He was the young music major who had taken over our youth choir and, among many other contributions to the district, had taught our choir of teenagers how to read music. We had been a team: he conducted, and I played the organ. We had a helpful chat. When he asked me if I had given any thought to the new retirement guideline, I realized that something needed to change. I was convinced the Church would not or could not change. I told him I'd give it some thought.

The possibility of retirement and the complaint, which came to my attention in a relatively short time, gave me pause. I had come to several conclusions as I watched from the sidelines while the last four years had crept by. First, I found it no longer easy or enjoyable to carry out my duties. Second, I was convinced that it would take decades to affect the changes. And third, if I did decide to stay, I would need to confront the leadership head-on and make some noise to get their attention. But there was no evidence that approach could work. Aside from getting me benched, confrontation would only frustrate me more. I was coming to think of myself as the problem rather than the solution.

I was exhausted. Years of effort now made me think of that oft-used definition of insanity: "Insanity is doing the same thing over and over again and expecting different results." I had compartmentalized the "interruptions" of Leonard Kolb Sr. and been satisfied to serve alongside Alex Klein. But that arrangement was a pacifier and after Klein's retirement, even though Bart Johnson had appreciated Klein as much as I did, I would not put up with the status quo any longer, not as a minister. The option to retire now appeared as a lifeline, even fifteen years prior to my sixty-fifth birthday.

It was time to take back my life. Beth agreed with me.

I called my immediate superior and my friend, District Evangelist Earl Buehner, who had recently been promoted. We met, and I shared my decision. "As soon as we can find a suitable replacement," I told him, "I would like to retire from my ministry." I had one person in mind, a deacon in another congregation. "Do you plan on leaving the Church?" Buehner asked me. Very observant, I thought. "I'm not sure yet," I replied. This meeting occurred in early 2004, perhaps in the spring. They could not arrange for the individual I had in mind to take my place, but I handed that decision off as of my meeting with Buehner, and by late summer, I had my retirement date on the calendar.

I would have preferred to finish what I had once started, had once vowed to give my life to. But people change. I certainly had. I had thrived for a while and with the help of Alex Klein, who encouraged such independence, had learned to think for myself. I remain convinced today that I made the best choice for myself and the congregations.

Rather than simply retire, however, today I sometimes wish I had resigned with a complete exit plan and a statement detailing why I was leaving the church. Nailing my reason on the door of the Church in Kitchener would have been a nice touch, making my reason for leaving unequivocal. I left because, first, I no longer had confidence in the Apostles' Ministry. It was a personal decision. Second, I was just too damaged to continue to care for anyone but myself. If anyone needed salvation, it was me. Third, others could follow my lead if so inclined. Anything I would have said might have detracted from the faith of those who were once under my care. I did not want to hurt anyone's feelings when I left the ministry, but such was the case, it was inevitable and unfortunate.

It soon became very clear to me that my decision, while stopping my personal pain, would leave me sitting in the pews of a church that no longer had anything to offer my soul. This was especially true regarding the content of the sermons. (I had considered this issue when I suggested the person I hoped would become my replacement.) What I needed from God was a challenge. A new challenge. It made sense to me to explore Christianity's wide selection of denominations. I had no desire to start another Church myself. To what end? As I learned a few months later, an Apostle from the Netherlands, after doing his best to negotiate a change in the circle of his own peers and for reasons we shared, had resigned, stating he would find a local church where he and his wife could continue their walk of faith.

16

Counting Rafters Again

That's a lot of rafters

Thanksgiving weekend 2004 was a four-day celebration beginning on Thursday with family and feast. The following Sunday morning, I sat in the sacristy for the last time as an ordained minister. Bart Johnson had asked me if I wanted to serve the congregation one last time before the retirement ceremony at the end of the service, and I had said yes. "Are you sure?" he'd asked me. "It can be quite an emotional moment." I said I thought I could handle it. But he was right. It was touch and go as I looked out over the packed church. Surprised to see some folks and disappointed in others, I understood more than most why some were missing. The words I shared that day have evaporated from my memory, but I do remember the faces I visited, each one a pin prick to my raw, exposed soul. I also recalled a smile, or a tear, we had shared over the years.

As if we hadn't already eaten enough that weekend, the congregation had planned a luncheon. I was still wearing my minister's hat, so to speak, when I went into the kitchen to check on why it was taking so long to get the food ready. I stepped on some toes while simultaneously remembering (a) that I was the guest of honor and (b) that my days of problem solving, especially in this kind of situation, were over. Scolding myself, I returned to sit with my wife and family.

I did not like my prospects of finding joy seated on those oak slabs as a member. I can imagine some people had pegged me as a choir member and would give me time to get used to my new role before nudging me to attend a choir practice or two. It never crossed my mind how boring my prospects were as most Sundays I had travelled to a different congregation to serve.

Having nothing to do before service now, I mostly sulked outdoors or in the car. Beth still needed to be at the church half an hour before the opening hymn as she was the organist most Sundays. And she sang in the choir. I wandered around the perimeter of the building, glad that my days of planning upkeep and hiring contractors to make repairs were in the rear-view mirror. In my mind, I reviewed the designs I'd come up with over the years to make the facility more useful. All that was someone else's problem now.

I really did not want to go in and sit down. The first time I walked through the doors of the foyer and not the sacristy, it hit me. Where do I want to sit? Of all the things that went through my mind, seating had not been high on the list. It turned out to be the first decision that made it all sink in. I sat alone toward the back, on the left side facing the altar, opposite the choir. No special reason. Less crowded, perhaps.

I have little memory of that first service or who conducted it, a man who may or may not have taken note of my new circumstance. I imagine I felt like a boy again, the seven-year-old who wandered off in search of distractions during most sermons. Yes, I was back to counting rafters. Sitting again in the Anaheim building, I studied the massive, laminated beams that the architect had designed to look like praying hands arching heavenward.

It only took one service to confirm what I feared: I would not be able to find what I was looking for. It had nothing to do with which of the ministers had drawn the short straw. This was just procedural, my mind confirming what I already knew. Finding a new spiritual home was the only way forward for me. I still believed, still wanted to follow Christ, and now I had something to occupy my time. What awaited me out there in the Christian world? Where would I start my search? I had not yet shared these thoughts with Beth. As the ministers each took their turns speaking, I started mentally sketching out a new future.

One thing I have now realized while revisiting those trying years was that I had buried a significant amount of righteous indignation. Four years earlier, when I had first considered an exit strategy, I had told myself it would not do me any good to leave the Church angry. I'd seen such anger before, and it was a common theme on the NAC board among those who had already left the Church. I also did not find a need to blame anyone but myself for my situation. When Alex Klein suggested that he had overstepped—and I'm not sure that's the correct way of putting it—when we thought he was trying to put the toothpaste back in the tube, I realized just how towering the "Emperor" was in his preferred suit of clothes. How powerful the Apostle's ministry was for those that were convinced they were Christ's ambassadors on earth. I, too, once held that conviction. But I was disappointed with the Church and its leadership, I felt let down and insignificant as an agent of change. My righteous indignation was not directed at the Church or at anyone else but myself. I should have realized the situation was impossible years before and spared myself the sorrow. Nothing had happened to me that suddenly demanded my departure.

17

Just a Stone's Throw

When at first you don't succeed…

We had driven past that church every Sunday for the last twenty-five years. I'd observed how their congregation had packed the original building to capacity. I'd watched as they broke ground on a new building that was five or six times bigger. Now I would get to see what it looked like inside that church. I calculated that I could have invited every NAC member of every congregation in California to this church and still had room for Oregon, Washington, Idaho, Nevada, and Arizona. Specifically, the entire West Coast District membership in attendance on any given Sunday.

Over the last few decades, I had scrubbed my mind of the belief that the NAC was the only Christian Church that could offer salvation.

My youngest son, confirmed half a year before my retirement, had accepted an invitation to visit a friend's church and had been attending there frequently. My conclusion was that there were more than enough Christian Churches through which salvation was available. I didn't need to start one. (This thought had crossed my mind in the same fashion as a falling star does when it breaches our atmosphere and disappears on the horizon.)

It was now the first or second week of the New Year, just over a month since my retirement. My need to find a church where I could breathe was imperative. It was time, and I asked Beth if she'd like to visit another church. "Just for fun?" "Not really," she said. "Okay then," I replied, "but I do. I think I'll go next service."

The following Sunday morning, I walked out my front door, one block over, and two down, jaywalking across Florence Avenue, over the curb and twenty feet to the doors of the Florence Avenue Foursquare Church (FAFC).

My dad had told me that he and a friend had once gone "to see what all the fuss was about" at Aimee Semple McPherson's Angelus Temple in Echo Park, just north of downtown Los Angeles. They would have been young ministers at the time, and Dad had said it was "just a curiosity." McPherson had founded the Foursquare denomination. I was "just curious," too. I had to dip my toes in somewhere to start. Why not right around the corner?

The FAFC offered two service times on Sunday mornings. They needed two (and later three) to accommodate all the members. Each service offered the same message. These were happy and welcoming people. I was overdressed and overwhelmed by the lively welcoming atmosphere. Nothing about my visit was off-putting. Was it possible that this was already the end of my search? I could not wait to bring Beth there to share what I felt. That Sunday morning, she had driven fifteen miles to attend at Anaheim without me. I wondered what she'd come up with if someone asked, "Where's Bill?" She played the organ and sang in the choir. Our kids were adults. Our two daughters both attended Anaheim with their husbands and children. We had a son away at UC San Diego, and our youngest son was at his friend's church. It was an ordinary, busy Sunday.

That morning, more than fifteen miles separated Beth and me. Just that thought was troubling.

When we met at our table for Sunday dinner, my excitement surprised her. What had become apparent to me almost instantly was the reality that my wife would need more time to process what I had already realized was my only option. I surprised even myself when I realized how easy it had been to take that first step away from the NAC. Now I hoped she could close the gap between my solution and her ongoing commitments without crashing our marriage. She had a front row seat, so to speak, as I agonized over my love-hate relationship with Leonard Kolb and as Alex Klein had dazzled us with his novel views and been there for all the drama. Beth had agreed that retirement was the right move for both of us.

The thought that I could blend back into the fabric of my old digs lasted all of ten seconds. And each time I returned to those pews a familiar feeling of dread drew near, walls closing in, freedom slipping away.

Just a few years before, also on a Sunday and on our way to Anaheim, I'd broached the subject of leaving the NAC with Beth. "If I would leave the Church," I'd asked, "would you come with me?" "Don't be so sure about that," she'd said.

***

Now I was poking around for land mines, hoping my life was not about to explode into little pieces. I had found my solution. In my mind, I'd left the Church already. But Beth had not considered retiring from her commitments in the congregation. I needed to review my reasons and help her see it from my point of view.

By retiring instead of resigning from the ministry, I handed back the tool given to me to serve souls. For me, retirement was part of honoring my original vow. Now I had lost respect for the ministry and, at that time, what it stood for, but not the men associated with it or the membership. And if I could not support that ministry, how could I pretend to continue in the

Church? It made no sense to even try. I was very lucky when Beth agreed to come with me to visit the Foursquare church. And I was so relieved when we both came away feeling that we'd found a new home.

Beth and I recently reminisced about that time. As she shared what it felt like to lay down the mantle of responsibility, I was reminded how important a role she'd played at my side while I was in the ministry. To say "we volunteered" would understate the investment that we'd made over decades of service. Service we did not regret. Saying we were unappreciated does not ring true. But today I wonder if some members did not consider us gluttons for punishment. There existed only a small nucleus of members that carried out the duties needed to keep a congregation up and running. No matter how often we asked for volunteers to sign up for the cleaning schedule or garden chores, it usually fell to that nucleus, mostly ministers and their wives, to keep the plates spinning.

After stealing away from her duties one morning and experiencing the same WOW factor I had felt at FAFC, it would still take a month for her to set down her responsibilities to join me permanently. Adopting our new church home, although no investment was being made yet, was like buying a profitable business rather than struggling with a startup. Even as a kid, I had wondered why my church did not grow as others did. It was hardly a startup, even though in the North American congregations it seemed to struggle as one. I was never proud of its standing in the Christian community. Now I was seeing firsthand what a prosperous congregation in my neighborhood looked like. What a thing it is to go from a struggling operation into a full-fledged success. And all we had to do was walk around the corner.

When Beth agreed we could find happiness at FAFC, my soul sighed in relief. We were free and our marriage was whole. *I* was whole.

My two daughters, both married and attending Anaheim, would have to make their own decisions. They soon realized, as did the rest of the congregation, that Beth and I would not be back. Our boys were on their own, too. One had a girlfriend he'd met at our Church, and he enjoyed the youth group near his campus. Our youngest son continued attending the church where his friend had made use of his exceptional musical talents in the praise band, something that the NAC was years from considering. They would all find their own way, of that, I was sure.

One day Earl Buehner invited Beth and me to join him and his dear wife for lunch. We had a pleasant conversation, after which he asked if we planned to come back to the NAC. I presented my new vista, what had now become our new reality, to Earl. "Probably not," I said, "If the Church (NAC) changes in the manner I hoped it might [I don't remember commenting about the time I thought that would take], then us coming back to Anaheim or any other congregation would amount to us changing congregations. By that time," I added, "there would be little difference between our beliefs, and new friendships would most likely prevail."

We would have preferred to remain friends with these dear people, but I just could not imagine how that would be possible. It was, and has been, the greatest sacrifice resulting from our decision. Many friends became old friends. Earl Buehner would become the first apostle ever to live in California. How could he find room for me in his world unless there was hope I'd concede?

The hope that all of Christianity could unite was one of my most naïve concepts, one which I carried with me when I left. I hoped that the Holy Spirit could lead all denominations into a common truth, one that would make the whole nearly impossible to tell apart. This concept of Christianity and what Christ had promised would, I hoped, unfold further, and I would make use of part of that logic at another point in my journey. I was coming to a turn in the road I could have never imagined.

Because our youngest was playing in the praise band at his new church, we visited his new spiritual home a few times before sinking our own roots. There was a different vibe there. It was small, and I had heard they were looking for a new pastor. A startup.

We had opted for the established and grand feel of a much larger and more diverse group of people, dipped our toes in, and were now ready to wade all the way in. We both enjoyed the Sunday morning stroll around the corner. There were several opportunities which called out to us, in the choir, adult Sunday School, and many men's and women's activities with the occasional pancake breakfast.

We met Terry Risser, the senior pastor, who welcomed us, explaining, "We're a conservative, Pentecostal congregation." Compared to the ruins of Kraus' autocracy I had just come from; I had not yet witnessed anything except a group of Christians living out their faith in a welcoming and down-to-earth manner. Several years later, the gist of Terry's political reference vis-a-vis conservatism would register with me, a frame of reference that my affiliation with the NAC had not provided. They were apolitical at the time.

For half a year following our departure, the NAC board provided a window through which I could monitor the scuttlebutt. That was how I found out about the Apostle from Europe who had left the NAC a month after me. He had chosen resignation. The Church had finagled a ceremony allowing it to officially take back its ministry. I could read the Apostle's letter online and that alone was worth the peek. Once an Apostle, he had come to the same conclusion I had. His extraordinary attempt to bring this to the highest leader in the Church, without finding a remedy, convinced me that change was still decades down the road. I had made the right decision for myself.

18

A Time for Healing

Who knew church could be so much fun?

"Hi, I'm Pastor Dave."

There was nothing subtle about the way we started attending our new neighborhood church. With a good deal of confidence, I led Beth to seats near the center of the main floor, which had four sections of seating below an equally wide balcony. I remember looking over my shoulder at her, my eyes twinkling, "You ready to take the plunge?" We sat on the aisle, three rows back from the front of the theater-like venue on Florence Avenue. It was nearly the exact place I had sat when I'd visited for my first time. I still wonder who may have accommodated us, the newcomers, who had taken their favored seats. The regular members definitely had their preferences. Were these two seats meant for us?

I was thrilled and relieved when Beth agreed to take a peek that first time, and, now after several visits, we both felt like we'd found a place to call home.

What is almost always true of things new in our lives is that we don't notice too many things out of place, not for a while, anyway. My normal need to observe, study, and think about a better way to do something never stirred. I could have noticed the choreography or the order of the service, but I didn't. I admired the level of commitment of the singers, their smiles, the joy which came from giving their talent.

For years as a minister in my old church, I had fought an urge to lift my hands, palms out, when I spoke the Benediction at the end of a sermon, something that would have landed me on the proverbial carpet back then. Here, I watched as prayer circles formed around a person in need. Hands were laid on the shoulders of the soul asking for intercession. This made sense to me. We were often invited to hold hands with those on either side of us during prayer.

Worship had never been more than a word used to describe pagans that bowed to other gods. Now it took on an entirely different scope, which was completely alien to Beth and me. Jeremy was the worship pastor, and it was his "calling" to lead the congregation in worship. He, along with the worship team, ushered us into a state of praise, acknowledgment, and purpose, reminding us why we had come together. Our hands held no hymnals. Lyrics appeared on a monitor, and we observed the surrounding believers lifting their arms toward heaven, directing their songs upward. This freedom allowed us to clap our hands when prompted, though this would take us a while to acclimate to, like the cold surf of the Pacific. As it is not in my nature to fake it, I held back from raising my arms for some time. Eventually, though, my hands slowly turned upward, then traveled farther from my sides until, like broken chains, I freed them. I found an acceptable, personal expression that fit my introverted self. But it took me months to warm to it. Shackled for so long, when I was set free to celebrate my faith in this manner, I wasn't sure how to go about it.

Otherwise, our transition into the fabric of Florence Avenue seemed fairly seamless. We poked our heads in on the many activities which served the various age groups there, and there were many to consider. Men's and women's groups had regular gatherings. It felt strange to be served and looked after, as before I had always been on the other side of the table, literally or mentally. The atmosphere was one of plenty as I met one potential friend after another. I wondered if this was what rehab was like. It was balm for my embattled soul. And even though I was well aware of the team behind the scenes stacking pancakes and delivering piles of them to the tables where hundreds of voices hummed as we kidded each other and shared stories, I allowed myself the luxury of being the one served. My first pancake breakfast ever. Saturday might have better uses, but I could not think of one that morning.

There were so many ways to socialize with our newfound brethren. Speakers, luncheons, dinners, the list was rich with opportunity. We were standing in line, waiting for the doors of the gym to open for one such occasion when Pastor Dave hugged us with his simple words of welcome, "Hi, I'm Pastor Dave." Then, as if it made perfect sense, he said, "There's a couple I'd like you to meet." Just a few feet away from us stood Tim and Sheri. We became quick friends. I don't know how Pastor Dave matched us to such a perfect couple. We crossed paths with them again when we came to choir practice. Sheri had a beautiful voice and served with the worship team. They both sang in the choir as we would, too.

Without ministerial duties, I found myself with a significant amount of extra time. I still had a business to run, I had no sermons to deliver or borders to cross, no hospital or family visits to make. After service, I no longer had to wonder who might ask if they could have a minute, or forty-five, to seek prayer or counsel.

Discretionary time is really a luxury, a commodity I now had in spades. But I did not regret the life of service which was now set aside. Satisfied that I had left my old denomination for the right reasons, I intended to survive as a Christian with my faith intact. I had not left the Savior. My retirement from the ministry and my departure from my childhood church were not a grab for some leisure time on my part. Like feeling a phantom limb, I missed being of service more than I had thought I would.

I wouldn't need to look far to fill that void. Like a rich kid raised to appreciate an excellent investment opportunity, I looked over my options. How could I serve? Where could I invest my time? In doing so, how could I reap the joy of giving?

Our hearts were beating in sync with the new body of Christ we had found. Adult Sunday School classes were held between the first and second services. We had chosen to attend the early service and had looked in on a few options before being welcomed into a class led by Pastor Dave's wife. Fellowship is a ubiquitous, transferable social practice, which is Christian code for social grazing, including donuts and similar fare. More importantly, and calorie-free, fellowship at our new church was a place to unburden myself. When I shared the struggle, I'd been through, I felt a rush of support. I did not need to go into detail about my journey. I found open, empathetic hearts. They invited me to lead the discussion from time to time. Another way to spend my time, and I still had plenty in the bank.

The very first time I had attended Florence Avenue Foursquare Church alone, the choir had sung. It was a practiced group singing four-part harmony. I observed during that first visit, and then when Beth joined me, that a transition was taking place in the music department. Even for a church that had roots in "that old-time religion," the music program was current with mainstream Christianity, which was unlike the hymns we had been singing since I was a child and which hailed from the 16th and 17th centuries.

My first visit alone may have been the last time their choir wore robes when they performed. On our next visit they appeared in business casual. Evidently, they only performed on one Sunday per month. The worship team was gaining popularity, and the church was adjusting to the trend. Adjusting to the trend...what a novel idea!

I would mourn the four-part choir, which I was told had at one time sung every Sunday. There are two perspectives to consider about four-part harmony. One is enjoyed as a singer and the other as a listener. Both embody the spirit of cooperation needed for any group of individuals to bring diverse ideas into a peaceful coexistence. It is a powerful tool that offers abundant rewards to all. Singing in a choir was one aspect of our old home church that meant a great deal to me, one that I had not enjoyed for nearly two decades. Music was a huge part of my life and inextricably connected to my sense of spirituality. There is something about harmonizing with groups of talented singers that lifts the human spirit. Love of music is a consummate love that combines intimacy, passion, and commitment. I have always found that whether the song was a spiritual or secular tune, the harmony was key. Music offers a unique setting where individuals can invest and realize beneficial returns. After we joined the choir at FAFC, it became apparent that it, too, was a fixture of the past and though there were those in the congregation that felt strongly about losing that connection to their past, they also had to accept the forward progress inspired by newer generations. It was a key characteristic of a church that knew how to thrive. Here I refer to those churches that were planning for a future and not being forced to manage an extinction event.

The opportunity to sing again in a choir was comforting to me. After I had become an evangelist in my old church, I'd had to give up singing in the men's choir. It was only once a month, if that, but I'd enjoyed singing with those men immensely. Our new choir mostly served on special occasions, and that was fine. I enjoyed interacting with the talented singers and gained more out of the rehearsals than I felt I'd put in. The drama and the music departments worked hand in hand and shared a large room dedicated to their activities. My skill set was put to work in both areas, which was quite gratifying.

Drama productions at my new church on Easter, Christmas, and the Fourth of July were elaborate. I enjoyed learning about and pitching in with set construction and design. All of my skills could be used in the process, including a solo in the musical at Christmas. I had never performed in a production like that before.

Once a month, I joined a group that took clothing and supplies to Skid Row in Los Angeles. The congregation owned a bus, and we would meet, load up, and head out. A merry band we were. Our guests at our destination were free to pick from the items available. But we offered more than the physical items we had on the bus. I observed my friends bringing the offer of Christ's salvation to those who were receptive, praying and listening to their concerns.

On one of these outings, I heard a new friend speak in tongues while he prayed with someone. This was a first for me in my new venue. Speaking in tongues is a uniquely Pentecostal practice and had never entered into the sermons or any other activities in my life so far, and I wasn't sure how I felt about it at the time. Most of the activities I participated in at FAFC did not resemble anything I'd been part of at my old church.

The satisfaction that I was experiencing was unusual for me. I was volunteering. My previous "participation" as a minister, although "voluntary," had carried with it a sense of duty, as if it was a paid position. There was a distinct sense of reward in my new endeavors. But one day, it occurred to me: I could return to ministry if I wanted to. The thought got as far as my "been-there, done-that" bin. Why mess up a good thing? I was still enjoying the cathartic effects of simple pleasures.

Our circle of friends at FAFC continued to grow. Our interests, like theirs, brought us together in the music room for rehearsals and other similar activities. When we discovered that the musician and the drama troupe met as a Sunday school class, it made sense to join them. This meant that we only had to walk down a hallway and into the music and drama room, instead of across campus, to access fellowship, aka the donuts. Dorothy Quertermous, affectionately known as Drama Mama, assistant pastor in charge of the drama department, led the group.

The Foursquare faith practiced baptism by full immersion. I had been baptized with water as an infant in my former church, and the next time the Apostle had visited, he had sealed me with the Holy Spirit, my parents accepting responsibility for my soul until my confirmation. Together those baptisms had represented two separate sacraments. Memories of my confirmation, the day I vowed to renounce Satan and serve God, left me with no significant sense of spiritual change, either. Well, I had hoped to kiss a girl later that day during a local home celebration of the event, but that was the extent of my Confirmation memory: a failed rendezvous.

I knew it was not required, but I asked Pastor Terry if it would be possible to be baptized again. The celebration helped me further mark the turning of that new page in my life and gave me a chance to invite my family to our new church home for the first time.

***

The first time I shared with Pastor Dave Englert what had brought me into their fellowship, he asked me to follow him into the sanctuary at Florence Avenue. There, he pointed to a specific pane of stained glass high up on the back wall. He wanted to share with me the significance of this panel. Their congregation, he told me, had received a prophecy regarding its future significance as a place of restorative grace and healing. He said that piece of art was a reminder for all to see. I could sense this was a profound part of his own connection to the congregation, and I can honestly say that I benefited from its directive during my time there.

Florence Avenue would be a layover on a journey I could not have imagined, as there was still a distance for me to travel. Alex Klein had christened my mode of transport, no pun intended. He had knocked my blinders off and even though I was still in that Platonic cave of sorts, the new perspective proved astonishing. But this was merely preparation for my continuing journey. Klein's counsel nudged me onto a path of personal discovery. Life, deaths, mentors from other walks and faiths, each became a part of my metamorphosis.

19

Looking Over My Shoulder

Remembering Lot's wife

Beth and I were both convinced that Florence Avenue was the answer we were looking for. That said, while I did my best not to dwell on the past, human nature is what it is, and I wanted to know what had occurred in the wake of our departure from the New Apostolic Church. Our daughters and their husbands still attended the Anaheim congregation, but I resisted asking them how the congregation was taking my departure. Or, in other words, how much were we missed? They wondered why those who said they missed us didn't call us and let us know themselves.

After ruminating about, and then ordering my priorities as to whether I should resign or retire, there was only one message I wanted to send to the leadership. I wanted to reiterate my disappointment and make it clear I had lost confidence in their ability to lead us to Christ. That was a personal belief I had come to hold. But I did not see any benefit in announcing that to the congregation. I had observed their faith in the matter and had no desire to become a wedge or to suggest a schism. I still thought I had done the best for the congregation and myself, considering the situation I found myself in. There were a few messages that let me know what I knew already, but you can't please everyone. I still had to pinch myself to see if what had occurred had not been one of those crazy realistic dreams that our brains conjure up.

Recently, I asked one of my daughters what she remembered about that time. She told me she had been left wondering what the hell had happened. "Dad raised us in this church," she'd told herself, "and now he ups and leaves." Years later, one of my sons-in-law told me it was very hard for him, too. He had just moved to California and experienced a surge in his faith. We had also welcomed him into our family, and he and I had a business relationship. We saw each other every day back then, and from what I remember, I shared some of my frustrations with him. But I did not sit down with any of my children and their spouses with the intention of sharing my deepest doubts about the Church. I wanted to provide them with the same "buffer" I believed was best for all of the members of the congregation.

I had adopted the attitude that if someone had a question; they had my phone number. Few members knew the personal toll those last years had exacted on me. And they could not know the relief I was now feeling after I'd left. In retrospect, I can understand how some members were merely respecting my privacy by not reaching out to me with questions.

While I regretted not resigning and saying my piece, I still think my decision was best for all concerned. Everyone is welcome to have their own opinions on this matter. I stand by mine.

My sister shared an interesting event that took place after my departure from the Church. At a luncheon following a service held by Apostle Leonard Kolb Jr., some of our family members had requested to meet with him to discuss my departure. She did not remember what had prompted the inquiry or what, if any, outcome might come out of that meeting. My sister and Beth's two sisters and their husbands were all present, and I think Earl Buehner and his wife were part of the conversation, too. The only thing my sister would share with me (other than that they'd had the meeting, and my leaving was the topic) was her own observation regarding my frame of mind: "He's never been happier in his life," she had told them.

A month or two after we had landed on our feet, one brave soul called me. I'd always admired her frankness. "Forgive me," she said, "but I need to know why you left the Church. There are rumors you left upset. Perhaps because they had passed you over for a higher ministry?" I explained to her that the only reason I had left was because I no longer agreed with the doctrine of the Church. "Thank you," she said, then, "All the best to you." And she hung up.

It made sense to me that some members might have thought that I'd left because I was passed over. Roughly a year before I retired, Earl Buehner, who had been a priest in Anaheim, had been promoted to district evangelist and my immediate superior. Those kinds of promotions always made heads turn. I was fine with his promotion, which signaled to me that my decision to reduce my activities had been interpreted correctly by the leadership.

Almost everyone left us alone. Even my parents did not inject themselves into our business as it related to matters of belief, past or present. I knew they were hurting. I also understood that my dad knew best what I was dealing with. He must have walked up to that fence and looked out over it himself, especially after Kraus took over. I imagined him cheering me on. At the same time, though, it would have been characteristic of the old-school mind-set for my parents to wonder if they were to blame in any way. But my father had witnessed the change that took place in me when Klein came into our lives, and he was there over all the decades during which we all struggled and waited for Klein's paradigm to change the whole church. Dad was present when the wind left my sails. There was nothing my parents did or could have done to change the scenario.

When we came together as a family, I never felt there were any elephants in the room. We joked, teased, and loved each other like always.

Well, our children were now adults, and they did make a few inquiries. Had they asked me for more information, I would have taken the time to explain my feelings. Eventually, they accepted my decision and I, theirs. My older daughter and her family continued to attend the NAC and still attend. Our other daughter and her family continued to attend in Anaheim, and then, after visiting some other churches closer to their home, they too left the NAC. My two sons would also find their own ways. The younger, in fact, had started his departure just a few months before Beth and I did.

From time to time in those early days, we would receive an invitation to a Christmas concert or hear that an old friend had passed away. Such events would bring us right back into the center of activity we once had been part of. Beth and I both had plenty of family still attending multiple congregations in the NAC. Some sang in the district choir, which still offered well-honed harmonies around the holidays. (If only the dogma could have evolved as much as the music program had over the years.) I'm sure that some folks, seeing us again in their company, wondered if we'd come to our senses. We had not. Funerals allowed us to say goodbye to old friends, people who had touched our lives, but were also a way to acknowledge that we once had shared life together and that they and their loved ones still held a place in our hearts. We had returned on these somber days to share life's true realities for a brief time. I wished I could have poured my heart out (like I'm doing in this book) to those whose only comment was "you are missed." These return visits were rare, however, and as the years added up, our presence at such events became more unusual. Like an old quilt, too fragile to handle, our past friendships remain a fond memory in our lives and always will. The beauty of that metaphorical quilt rests nearby.

The continued development of social media and the internet made it easy for me to get a glimpse into my old world from time to time. I browsed online to see how life was unfolding for old friends. Both Beth and I posted pictures as evidence that we still had a life. Over the years, I would observe a younger generation, my children's contemporaries, maintaining their friendships even though some of them had chosen another denomination. Or none. This was heartening. Even ministers of their generation made efforts to accommodate their old friends. That was good to see.

20

A Mulligan

You want to do what?

Walking down the aisle alone on my first visit to the Florence Avenue Foursquare Church, was a rush. I did so with no inhibitions, as if I were coming home. The usher had just nodded, as if he knew where I was going. I wondered if I were sitting in a seat a regular member had staked out. Because it was my intention to immerse myself fully into the experience, I sat on the aisle near the front of the church.

All of the early memories I have of our immersion into the fellowship at FAFC have to do with a feeling of relief and having found a safe harbor. While there were so many diverse activities that we took part in, some stand out, namely, opportunities to serve others. Although it seemed like four or five years had passed before the idea of returning to the ministry became a frequent visitor in my thoughts, it only took two years before, once again, I found myself standing on the brink of another set of rapids, my adrenaline pumping. I was excited by the possibilities. This time, entering the ministry could be different. It could give me the chance to attend seminary, something I had believed the NAC should have instituted decades ago. The thought of studying the scripture and the life of Christ in greater detail appealed to me very much. I also believed that I still had something to offer the cause.

I'd lived in my old Platonic cave for fifty years, and from my birth it had seemed I'd been predestined to serve. My life was defined by my heritage and all of the implications attributed to the Church and the beliefs of our people. To say that much had changed would be a grand understatement. I was so immersed in my new cave that my past seemed like a mere dream.

My activities at FAFC continued expanding. I connected with another associate pastor named Joe, who cared for the senior members in the congregation. Joe invited me to join him on home and hospital visits. Once he got to know me, he asked if I'd like to make visits on my own. I said yes and began visiting members in the hospital. Joe and I became friends. He introduced me to the Pinks hot-dog stand, a famous joint in Hollywood frequented by tinsel town elites. (That's right—fifty years in Los Angeles had not introduced me to the best dogs in town.) I enjoyed hanging out with Joe and during one of our outings asked him what he thought of my becoming a minister again. He was quiet for a bit, then he said, "I was told once that that's something you should feel you're being dragged into, kicking and screaming." That reply somehow did not register with me. I said I'd have to give it some thought.

Ministry, in my experience in the NAC, lacked any of the drama Joe had hinted at. My induction into the ministry had begun when I was a child and, because as a teen I felt little choice in the matter, I considered it something I would have to endure. It was an awkward combination of growing pains and great expectations on the part of my parents and a watchful congregation. I imagine that there are few fourteen-year-olds that would not become anxious learning to speak in public. I did not feel it was the Lord pulling me into his service. Today I would say it amounted to social pressure. All my kicking and screaming during those traumatizing teenage years occurred in my head. My anxiety while "learning" to speak extemporaneously from the altar was palpable. It felt more like I was being held down, told not to complain while enduring hazing. A barricade of faithful ministers was standing at all but one door. With no one to speak to and no way to interpret my feelings, I convinced myself I had to do this to make my family proud. Before I knew it, I was kneeling before an Apostle who ordained me. At some point it became a source of pride on my part and then my ego joined in for the rest of the journey. Anxiety was part of growing up.

Returning to ministry as a liberated adult presented a new set of scenarios. This opportunity included a salary. At the time, such a perk would have both been an answer to my financial needs and possibly the opposite of what my soul needed. The last thing I wanted the ministry to represent was merely a way to earn a living.

After struggling to stay profitable for several years, the pattern shop fell on hard times and because I was unwilling to file for bankruptcy, I arranged to reorganize my debts. Part of that process included selling machinery no longer needed and repurposing the wood shop to design and build custom furniture. I had also been doing some remodeling work which looked promising and was considering getting a contractor's license. By then we were doing fine financially and hoping to do better. But progress would take some time. The challenge to start and grow a new company was substantial and I wasn't getting any younger. I was designing and building furniture, custom cabinets, and taking on remodeling jobs all on my own, and feeling the work in every limb and sinew of my creaking, fifty-something body. I wasn't sure if I'd be able to carry the load by myself long enough to build a clientele and hire a crew. I also still needed to get a contractor's license to make the business legit.

I was catching up with an old friend, an ex-minister who had also left the NAC, and bounced the idea of returning to ministry off him. He thought about it differently. At first, I chortled at his take on the idea, which was "showing my old comrades in the NAC that I could land on my feet and continue in the ministry." I had the dickens of a time putting that idea to rest. I did not want showing off to be my motivation. No, I was making a new start. This I would do for myself out of a genuine desire to serve.

Beth did not think returning to the ministry was a good idea for me.

I really enjoyed speaking about the Gospel and leading an occasional Sunday School discussion. The old days of tortured youth services were long gone, and now I actually enjoyed speaking, especially extemporaneously. Nothing to commit to memory!

And my ego was elbowing me, too. There was a certain prestige that ministry afforded and which I missed, and it was that aspect that stood out to me as the biggest red flag in my deliberations. An old itch that I still felt conflicted about. But who was I kidding? We should all take pride in our career choices. I had never considered ministry a career.

While I juggled the pros and cons of returning to ministry, part of me insisted I stay positive. I visited the seminary's website and imagined myself as a student. It meant nearly four years of schooling ahead. It wouldn't be cheap, either. But, I learned, ordination was possible before completing the schooling. In fact, I was told that I had plenty of experience, as evidenced already, enough to skip the schooling. It was not a requirement. But the seminary was what attracted me the most at the time.

Becoming a minister in a new denomination I was still learning about would have its challenges, too. As a member, I still had the ability to pick and choose from ideas I found different from my own interpretations of the Scriptures, and I had already been rebuffed when I introduced ideas from Scripture that did not fit the Foursquare brand, if I could call it that. In some ways I was challenging their belief that the Bible was immutable.

What I did not appreciate at the time, and this was one of Beth's points, was that I was already giving one hundred percent, if not more, in service to others. And I was very content doing this. Returning to the ministry would, in this case, mean something altogether different. It amounted to a real job and a paycheck and a boss, plus acceptance of a specific list of beliefs, the definition of a denomination. Whereas in my former Church the distinction between the two masters before me, God and Church, were synonymous in my mind, here in the Foursquare denomination, the church was a business entity and the concept of salvation came down to a personal relationship with Christ which did not require the authority figure of a Church to regulate or reign over it.

Caught up in the vibrant charisma of my new Church family, I may have been choosing the ministry as a way to prove to myself and to my new and old Church families that my faith was still alive and active. The appeal to express faith by works was a way of breathing some sort of physical dimension into the unknown and unseen.

Another aspect of the ministry, which I had experienced differently in my teens, was being called versus volunteering. Jesus called (invited) his disciples (in Matthew 19: 21) to follow him. When a rich ruler inquired about being of service, Christ challenged him, telling him to first sell all that he had, and then come and follow him, but the man was too rich to make the deal. I'm not sure if what had originally brought me into ministry could qualify as a calling, but I know I did not volunteer. This time around, I questioned if my motives were aboveboard. Was I volunteering? This probably amounted to the baggage I was still carrying from my past life.

Joe and I had many opportunities to discuss my future. He was aware of my level of service prior to meeting him and was interested in my opinion of ministers who received remunerations for their service. I told him I had wished many times that I could have been a full-time minister without the need to have a secular job. Joe, in turn, shared his own thoughts on serving without pay versus the "stigma" of getting paid for that service. I came back to him after thinking about the idea a bit more. I had plenty of personal experience from the last two decades, and I felt there were two aspects of service that I believed at the time could benefit from being a salaried minister.

One aspect was the focus required to dedicate a life to God's kingdom on earth. My own experience with traveling in Mexico had proved quite challenging. After spending two weeks focused only on Church matters, I would come home to my business and have trouble refocusing on that operation. The project I was working on in Mexico had grown from simple trips spent inviting and testifying to include the added weight of responsibility I felt, which was to care for souls there, including the two evangelists that lived there and were employed by the Church full-time. It was part of my work to create a plan and suggest how to proceed, to coordinate all of those aspects with those two evangelists, and to present a plan to Kolb and Klein for their approval. Add to that, I felt the same desire to realize prosperity in several congregations assigned to me in Los Angeles. Tucked in between all of that work was my family life, the hands of my wife and my four children slipping in and out of mine whenever possible.

The second point I wanted to make to Joe was the need to understand the Scriptures. There are plenty of biblical authors, each with a slightly different approach to Christ's message. It takes time to ponder these various accounts, and I saw the benefit of having time for such consideration. If the average person does not have the time to discern the depths of the Scriptures, would it not fall to those who dedicate their lives in this manner to do so on their behalf? This was a theory inspired by a recent event in my life on the shores of a beautiful lake.

I was leading an adult Sunday School class when I shared what I had experienced on the shore of that lake. "We were up at our usual vacation spot, a small lake in central Idaho," I said. "I had come down to the beach to read. It was after lunch and the usual strong breeze had picked up, coming off the lake. There were a couple of kites struggling in a strong gale and bringing smiles to a couple of kids at the end of the boat dock. The wind had churned up the water too, and relatively enormous waves were crashing on the shore, beating on the boats. A line and pulley clanged against a sailboat mast. I thought of Christ in the storm," I continued, "and how he had calmed the wind. For several days, I had been doing little but contemplating matters of the soul and felt a peace come over me. I thought to myself, Why not? *Peace, be still*, I said under my breath, intentionally willing the rushing air to calm. The kites just fell out of the sky. Instantly there was calm and not just for a moment. The winds had ceased. I said nothing to anyone on the beach." Giving my audience a minute to absorb my story, I added one caveat. "It could have been that I was just so at peace, having time to reflect on the beauty of God's creation, that this thing happened. That it was possible because I was so removed from life's many distractions." I was implying that Christ had mastered and could easily access the discipline to harness such a power.

The class went silent, then someone spoke up and said, "I have goosebumps!" I did, too. I had not made up that story. It had happened exactly as I'd related it. (Well, there may have been three kites.) I had spoken the words in my head while sitting, relaxing in my seat. I resumed reading, curious about what had happened. The next day, around the same time, the same gusty winds had picked up, equally annoying. I repeated the words, now an experiment. "*Peace, be still.*" The winds smiled as they rushed past my ears and flapped the pages of my book. Another day on the lake, another human that thought he had some gift.

That single event fueled my tentative theory about the benefits of dedicating one's life to contemplating God's Kingdom.

This was not the first time in my life when I might have thought I'd brushed up against some paranormal presence at work in my life.

Earlier, as a young man still living at home, I had been out driving somewhere and navigating a four-way stop. I looked both ways. Everything looked clear. My hand had moved the column shifter to first gear, I was ready to continue when my foot slipped off the clutch of my old '67 Chevy pickup. The beast lurched a foot and stalled. On my left I sensed movement, and when I looked over, a car which would have T-boned me, blew through the stop sign. It was coming down a rather steep hill, and fast. I've always considered that moment as a coincidence.

On another occasion, it was after work on a weekday, and I had been helping to set up a rented auditorium for an Apostle service. Ernst Streck-eisen, a Swiss Apostle and future Chief Apostle was conducting the service that evening. They had assigned me to be an usher for the service. Exhaust-ed from the rush to set up, I found a seat to rest in. I had been sitting for a good amount of time, letting the many other ushers look smart, when, about midway in the sermon, in a trance-like stillness I felt my body rising from my chair. My entire body just hovered there for an undetermined time. I remember looking at the minister and other fixtures in the room to try to orient myself...and then, I was back in bodily contact with the seat again. When I later shared this event with my psychologist, he told me that this sensation can be experienced after staying perfectly still for a long period. It is a form of vertigo. And he left it at that.

So there you go. Unusual moments in the life of a person in search of evidence not seen. Or repeatable. Events which could easily be interpreted as otherworldly.

Throughout my life, the boy who wanted to believe with all his heart had wondered why the apostles in his boyhood church could not pull off the miracles of which the Bible suggests they should be capable of. I have felt that maybe, like some mad scientist, I would be the one that gained whatever power it was that had eluded these distinguished men. The best they could do was find stories that suggested somehow that God looked after His own. This was the story from one of those Apostles as he spoke of a minister in *"our church"* (the NAC) who was let go from his job on a Friday. He was called back on Monday because of the death of another employee over the weekend.

It truly is amazing what the human mind will allow itself to believe in order to justify an imagined preeminence. A senior Apostle shared this *miracle* in a nationally televised broadcast. I'm sure our Church was not the only group of believers that felt their lives were favored by God.

***

Mom and Dad moved from Southern California to Boise, Idaho, as soon as he retired from the ministry. It had been a lifelong dream of his to live in a smaller town. He had wanted a five-acre farm, but Mom convinced him to settle for a home in town. My sister and her family lived nearby. About three years later, I retired from ministry and then left the church (NAC). Two years after that, Mom called with some news. Dad's doctor had confirmed that he had Alzheimer's, something we had begun to suspect. She added that they laughed and cried plenty.

One thing I had observed and learned from my new Church family was the aggressive posture they took against illness. The next time I visited my dad after hearing of his illness, I told him, in no uncertain terms, "This does not have to be your story, Dad." My belief in the power of God to cure illness had fine-tuned my prayers, which were now more direct, specific, and inspired. I steeled my heart against the prognosis and decided I could command a different outcome from this diagnosis.

The Pentecostal zeal of my new tribe was contagious. In my life of faith, I preferred action. Doing and manifesting in metaphysical terms. This had been my response to dark clouds. Find something to do to express my faith. In this case, like so many others, my posturing would be tantamount to treading water, the opposite of walking on water and what I was imagining my supercharged faith could make happen.

***

I asked to meet with Terry Risser, the senior pastor at Florence Avenue, to discuss becoming a minister in the Foursquare denomination. He told me that my life experience was qualification enough, but the idea of going to seminary still greatly appealed to me. Whether or not a degree was required in this case, it was something I wanted in my toolkit. So Terry prepared an application for me and attached his personal evaluation as my senior pastor. I do not recall how much time passed, but an approval followed. Then there would be an undetermined waiting period before they would enroll me in a polity course that would lead to licensing. I inquired about Life Pacific University, a private Bible college endorsed by the International Foursquare denomination. It would cost $11,000 a year. My plan was to first return to finish my Associate of Arts (AA)degree at Cerritos Community College, which I could afford, and then transfer to Life Pacific and figure out the financing later.

Yes, my work alongside Joe had me thinking as a minister again. I suggested an idea to bring smaller groups together for more intimate spiritual conversations, meeting in people's homes, and using suggested topics for discussion. Terry Risser offered me a *limited* part-time position at Florence

Avenue as the small group coordinator. I was surprised by the offer and the wage, not sure if it was a prelude to a permanent position.

Terry later told me that he had assumed I would want a church or congregation of my own. I was not exactly sure about that, as I was still exploring all the possibilities. The small group idea did not catch on, however, and the position trickled away. The employment experience was a disappointment, not what I had expected it would be. Or become. Something about it, perhaps having a boss after so many years of self-employment, just did not sit well with me. Not to worry, though. I was still quite busy with small construction and custom furniture projects which would allow me the flexible hours needed to pursue my future classwork. I saw a counselor at Cerritos Community College and arranged for my previous credits, earned in 1972 at Glendale Community College, to be verified and transferred. I began classes in January, opening the spring semester of 2007.

The support I was receiving at Florence Avenue strongly encouraged me, even though I was not sure how, or if, I would experience "being dragged kicking and screaming" into my new profession. It was still early, and I had a way to go, but I was excited to see what this new chapter of my life might offer.

21

A Midlife Dream

Old enough to know better

You might think that at age fifty-three, I would have ironed out all those pesky religious doubts long ago. Now I was approaching the prospect of education and a new start in the ministry feeling like a guy on his way to a prime rib dinner. I saw that as a fairly good sign that my mind was in step with its decision to pursue ministry.

For the past twenty years, give or take, I had practiced my faith based on an understanding of Scriptures that stressed the life of Christ and the ideal kingdom he had established on earth. Now I was returning to college intending to achieve a bachelor's degree and possibly a Ph.D. which I would use in a new ministry.

Looking back as I write this book and at the significance of this next chapter in my life, I picture myself arriving at college with a briefcase packed with doubts that had traveled with me for my entire life. It was clear on my first day on campus that I would never blend in fashion-wise. I arrived with an old briefcase to carry my books and assignments on campus, the kids probably thought I was a professor. My religious doubts, however, were voluminous and stored in that room in my head, down the hall from the chapel in my mind. I do not know at what age I began comparing what I heard in Church to that other voice in my head, common sense, perhaps, but I was young. That extra room allowed me to compartmentalize the scraps of empirical knowledge I'd ponder and did not fit in with my religious paradigm growing up. Those doubts represented an entirely different picture and did not belong in the same box as the picture of my life up to that point. Jigsaw puzzles are challenging enough without mixing pieces from two in the same box.

I may have been subconsciously taking this collection with me to present to those I would meet at college, the learned and the wise, hoping they could make sense of my collection. And if they scratched their heads and could not offer answers, maybe the faculty at the seminary would be up to the task. Perhaps they could lay my puzzles to rest. As my education proceeded, I would reference every mental note I'd tucked away, every doubt I had about my take on God and His Creation. I had taken this dissonant collection with me everywhere I'd been. After my first enlightenment, when the Gospels came to life, I began to wonder, what else did I get wrong? This was a recurring thought and a plausible threat to my future as a Christian, and especially as a minister.

Before I left the NAC, I had cleaned out some of those old scraps of doubt, primarily because they were no longer doubts but tools which I had used to free myself of the old logic and the old dogma. I arrived at FAFC with a burning desire to continue my discipleship, and to do so with fewer past doubts, though there were still plenty of them remaining in my mind. In that way, I was like every other Christian striving to make sense of life's tragedies while testifying to God's magnanimous love.

Does God exist? Even the most general inquiry can be quite complex. One question I had not shaken, and probably never would, was this: Why was a two-year-old child struck down with cancer? This experience was high on my list of things I found hard to comprehend, and although I attempted to comfort the mother of this beautiful little girl and conduct her funeral, I felt it was really a task for God Himself. To this day, I'm not sure where He was as I waded into the abyss that was created by the girl's passing. At her funeral, which was packed with mourners, I was numb. I might as well have worn a jester's hat and danced around the altar for all the help I wanted to offer but lacked.

When my brother passed away in a freak accident at age thirty-four, the most comforting words I heard from my then-favorite mentor were "Shit happens." That seemed to make sense, as it did with most tragedies in life. But where does this profound observation fit into a life of faith? My mother still tries to fit what happened to her son into a category I simply disdain: "Everything happens for a reason." When Alex Klein's brother also died in an accident not long after my brother's death, I often wondered if Klein would frame his experience with the same words, "shit happens."

Over a lifetime of sorrows, how can a believer be expected to recover from incomprehensible losses? There are many clichés that reference such afflictions as character builders, as means to strengthen one's faith. Loss is definitely a test of faith, yes, but it is not necessarily a test to prove God exists outside the mind of the believing soul.

In my experience, when we suspend faith or it fails us, it is restored because we make the choice or renew our choice to believe. Maybe this is because it is easier than arguing with the pious or with oneself. Or maybe it somehow provides a way to place the painful event behind us. We may think of it as our way of having passed through a time of tribulation, but if we desire to believe, we must be prepared to set reason aside.

Reason and knowledge are tangibles that do not easily fit into matters of faith. This paradox is also a part of my experience. All the personal adjusting, though, does not address the thing that happened or explain an omniscient God's footprint. Most of the time, the promise of life eternal or the fear of hell—the two grand premises of Christianity—prevail, and hoping for the best, we rejoin the pilgrims. Another port in a storm, and it's a huge one, is family. I often used the fear of disappointing my family as a bridge back to faith. Rather than disappoint them, I borrowed their faith until I was back in my trance.

If I were a pathologist presiding over the postmortem of myself as a Christian, I would pause when I came across the next chapter in my life.

22

A Curious Mind

Wait a minute—it's okay to challenge authority?

Can you recall the smell of blue jeans piled up high in the department store at the start of a new school year? When I was a kid, I always looked forward to going back to school. It may have been that smell, or maybe it was the promise of crisp fall air after a stifling summer. Or it may have been the opportunity to explore a world outside my Platonic cave. When I saw what passed for college haute couture, thirty-four years after my last go at college, my jaw dropped.

My first semester in college began in January 2007. I was especially excited about the philosophy and astrobiology courses I'd signed up for. (Apologies to my journalism and speech class professors.) My philosophy professor, who was head of the department, introduced himself as a Christian Existentialist. I did not know what that meant, but at least, I understood he was a theist. At a certain point, he inquired about our reasons for taking his class. Looking as far ahead as I dared, I presented my grand plan. "I'm here to finish my AA," I told him, "and then I'll transfer to seminary. Lately I've been considering pursuing a doctorate. I'd like to build a bridge linking religion and science."

Sharing my vision with the head of the philosophy department would prove fortuitous. Upon graduation, I received the department's award for academic excellence. But putting my thoughts together in the same statement had also shone a light on a growing personal need in my life.

This was a need that was about to come to the front of my belief system and require my full attention. I would have to reconcile my ongoing mental debate about science and religion before I could dream of building a bridge between them.

Philosophy 101 provided a foundation for the intellectual journey I was setting out on. Combined with the daily journaling assignment, the class became an anchor for me as I adjusted to the rigors of classwork. The course offered insights into the minds of the greatest thinkers the world has known, and each session introduced a new selection of words related to the subject, which provided me useful ways of organizing and categorizing my thoughts. Revisiting my journal notes today, I read about days where lofty thoughts bore me away from the mundane, also days where the realist in me grounded me at work in the shop, where I still had clients and orders to fill. The key ideas of the major philosophers were at my fingertips and the question I asked myself, after Alex Klein had shown me another way to think about my Church, presented itself again. What else did I get wrong?

I hit it off with the philosophy professor, whose side gig was woodworking. When he boasted of having a contractor's license, I said that was something I had been considering acquiring myself. We often stopped to chat after class, and one day he suggested I might be interested in the local Theosophical Society, where he occasionally gave talks. There too, he told me, I would find ideas that were similar to mine yet new. I shared my story with him about how I ended up at FAFC. I appreciated his considerate response, the gist of which was that he had "certain expectations of the subjects presented when attending religious gatherings." This was a generous detail that allowed me to reflect on another man's epistemological standards relative to my own. Moments like these were gold and contributed to my quest.

I cannot imagine myself pursuing knowledge with such abandon and hunger before I entered my thirties. While I was enjoying the respite from my old digs, and Florence Avenue was still holding my attention, this new scholarly venue was scintillating.

My class in astrobiology promised a paradigm as vast as the universe itself. I asked my professor how the course compared to *A Briefer History of Time* by Stephen Hawking and others. Her answer: "It will expand and go beyond." Perched atop a desk, her legs crossed like a guru's, she clarified the difference between astronomy and astrology. That was a sad commentary regarding my fellow students, but why she needed to explain the difference would become clear.

At my age, it was difficult to gauge the ages of my fellow students. I would never have thought that pajamas would be a suitable clothing choice for college. And why a professor would not wake a student determined to sleep through an entire class also left me speechless. But here I was observing an unusual number of listless teenagers. I was told they were hiding from their parents in the only place that would secure their allowance and a roof to shelter their toys. Because of privacy laws, their parents could not access their grades or any personal records. Some parents were being bamboozled.

This professor made one more point before we cracked the books. "There will be no references to any giant turtles allowed in this class." I'm pretty sure she was talking to me, as I knew she was referring to the opening chapter of Hawking's book, in which he recalled a public lecture he thought might have been given by Bertrand Russell. As the lecturer described the universe, a "little old lady" called him out: "What you have told us is rubbish. The world is a flat plate supported on the back of a giant turtle." When asked what the turtle was standing on, the lady made it perfectly clear. "It's turtles all the way down!" I interpreted the professor's comment about turtles as a warning. There would be no room for super-fluous ideas about the subject being presented. I had shared my plans and how the courses I was taking served as a stepping block to the seminary and ministry. It may have been my first test. Had I read Hawking's book?

It is interesting that now, as I write this, I see a relationship between this professor of astrobiology and Alex Klein. Two excellent teachers, both presenting subjects that dwarfed both instructor and student, leaving us all in awe of something that was beyond our reach. But both of these teachers were issuing a license to query knowledge, to learn how to fish as opposed to just accepting what you were being fed.

It's hard for me to imagine that anyone living now and reading these words will ever know the complete story of the universe. I would venture a guess that our species may never hold all of the mysteries in its knowledge base. There is simply too much to know. We can only relish what our own experience in life holds, relative to our current knowledge.

I was never a fan of the days when a teacher wheeled a TV monitor into the classroom. Substitutes might get away with it, but this was our full-time astronomy professor slipping a documentary DVD into the ma-chine. The purpose? To bring anyone awake on a unique journey. In the simplest terms, it was a lesson in relativity, though not the kind made fa-mous by Einstein, although he made several appearances in future lessons.

Even though we watched this presentation on a thirty-six-inch tube television, the subject matter kept me in goosebumps, transporting me, a single human, to multiple points of view, all relative to my place in the width and breadth of the universe. Who am I, who are we, relative to that expanse?

Transported by cameras, microscopes, and telescopes we journeyed to the quantum level and, with clever references and cinematography, zoomed out and up from these, the tiniest, pieces of the discoverable world.

The components, atoms, elements, and compounds expanded and congealed, acquiring complexity until after a whirlwind journey, they briefly exposed what the naked eye can observe as we stroll through life. The journey resumed, and using the latest scientific instruments, we leapt a foot, then a mile, until we reached the speed of light, traveling as Einstein had once imagined in a thought experiment, as companions alongside a wave of light. Eons passed as different forms on the spectrum of light delivered evidence of what the human eye could not see. Measuring the age of the universe relative to the time it took ancient photons to report back to one's optical nerve transformed me and my classmates into insignificant specks compared to the exponential distance that separated us from the brink of creation, the Big Bang. Together, we arrived just a split second before everything began and the conditions allowing a photon (light) to exist were not yet in place. That would come 250,000 or 300,000 years later.

Once more in my life, someone, some thing, had throttled my perspective. This summoned my full attention. Not just profound, this comprehensive panorama was life changing and when it ended, left me with an existential presence I could not have imagined before. I felt like a kindergartener as I tried to share this with my wife at dinner that evening. I still find it impossible to convey in mere words.

In this single college course, we would learn about the physical laws which existed in the universe, or multiverse, rules allowing one element to dance, or collide with one, but not another, or only if certain conditions existed. The sequence of events based on natural laws and the building blocks that resulted from the Big Bang, 13.8 billion years earlier, laid the foundation for areas of study such as physics, chemistry, biology, etc., not to mention the evolutionary process resulting in our *Homo sapiens* mind. Equipped with this mind, humanity could observe the night sky and contemplate our place in the universe. We can literally look back 13 billion years and see time unfolding, reality forming, and, when we pause to look in the mirror and observe our individual footprint, gain a unique perspective which shows us just how brief and recent our presence as a species compares to the whole.

You might wonder, after all of this poured over my soul, did I still believe in God? Yes, I did. I would have declared that it was high time we theists brought such obvious knowledge across my imaginary bridge and onto our island. I now had specific information that I could include in constructing that doctoral thesis which I told my philosophy professor about (a bridge between science and religion). Never a literalist in the biblical sense, I hoped to accommodate both realities and wanted to get science and religion to shake hands on a compromise. But here I must be practical. There is no single island called Christianity. It is more like an archipelago and some of those religious communities, I would soon learn, already had made room for evolution and the Big Bang in their own belief systems. I still had much to learn.

What was it that set off the Big Bang, the singularity from which everything we know came to be? Why not God? Is God not a singularity? A whole segment of Christianity would disagree with this idea. For if I were to consider that Big Bang singularity as God, well, then I'd have to consider a concept of such a God from scratch. This would not be the first time that a man described an unknown phenomenon as a deity or changed a previous concept of a deity to fit a particular idea. It would be an unknowable entity. Such were this philosopher's thoughts on the subject. I concluded *Who the f#%k knows?* (A new title for this book perhaps...?)

One thing I have learned is that a man can stand on the mountaintop gazing at the valleys, distant peaks, and every other feature in a panorama and get nowhere, fast. Me, I needed to decide. Pick a trail, Bill. Walk it, enjoy the scenery, and focus on the path ahead.

It's been said that we all die alone. That is a part of life I have witnessed. Even if we're surrounded by medical staff or family, we each and alone face and see our death uniquely. We could say the same for our birth. We all come into the world similarly, but not one of us is alike. Even twins see each other differently and are therefore two unique persons.

And then there was me...on the brink of rebirth into a world without a god. I took note of everything that was conspiring to deliver me out of the past and drag me, kicking and screaming, into the future.

And that was how the clouds on my horizon were changing, how what I could see was evolving into different shapes. I had been observing panoramas that were too vast, too homogenized. Stepping out of my Platonic cave, I was now observing and acknowledging a vast spectrum of religious belief supported by all levels and manifestations of faith. Some believers meditated, while others persecuted the infidel. Scientists were building massive instruments that collided unseen particles one into the other, revealing the predicted secrets they held. Astronomers collected photons that had traveled billions of light years to share their wonder. None of this had anything to do with a virgin birth. The one big difference between the religious and scientific vistas was that the natural world was revealing knowledge that was tangible, measurable, and repeatable.

My palate for knowledge was more refined than I had given it credit for, but, like my philosophy professor said, it was critical that I vet the value and provenance of the knowledge I was collecting. I was acquiring information that was crucial to my search for answers regarding the state of my faith in God.

This was shaping up to be a final stand. I decided to do whatever it took on my part to consider every source of knowledge the world had to offer, and for the first time in my life I had to accept that I was the only one whose opinion mattered to me in my quest. It was my mind, my soul, if you will, that needed to find a logical and informed map for my continuing journey on this planet. Faith was a well-worn path, but more and more, I felt I had seen all it had to offer.

Another trail beckoned to me.

23

A Beer and a Sausage

Prost!

Glossolalia, a *heavenly language* referred to in the New Testament as speaking in tongues, is a peculiar spiritual gift which had never been a part of my Christian experience in my old church, but I did witness a few members and ministers at the Florence Avenue Foursquare Church interjecting a bit of the *heavenly language* (the preferred term at FAFC) into a prayer. It was like grabbing a pinch of salt for a bubbling stew, but its use was not prolific.

According to the New Testament, the believers present at the first Christian Pentecost were not all locals and did not all speak the same language. They had gathered for Shavuot (a Jewish festival) and were "miraculously" able to hear what the original Apostles were saying in their own languages even though the apostles were all Galileans and spoke only one language. I had believed this demonstration as recorded in Scripture (Acts 2:6-7) to be a special dispensation unique to the first Pentecost.

St. Paul also addressed the use of this "gift" in I Corinthians 14. But his account suggests another type of communication, which in the secular world is referred to as glossolalia. He also stressed the importance of interpreting such "language" if it were to be of any value to the church. Glossolalia is prominent in Pentecostal faiths, but while there have been scientific studies made to compare the recorded sounds of those who claim they are speaking in tongues, those studies find no relation to modern or known ancient languages. The studies also could not distinguish a structure that would suggest that the sounds are any kind of language at all.

Before I came to FAFC, I had heard believers speak in tongues at various churches. This was during a time when someone in the NAC had the bold idea to attempt wholesale proselytizing. The idea was to convert the minister, expecting that the congregation would follow. I had never considered the phenomena of speaking in tongues as useful, however, whether for communicating or as proof of the Holy Spirit's presence.

It was announced that a husband and wife team would come to speak at Florence Avenue on "the gift of speaking in tongues." Shortly before this event, Joe Jenkins had spoken with me about the gift of a heavenly language and the benefit of this gift for the ministry. When I spoke with Joe more recently, however, to clear up some of my memories regarding Foursquare policy and the need to possess this gift as a requirement to enter the ministry, he corrected me, saying it was not a requirement. I was always an overachiever when it came to having the right tools for a job, something I had learned as a craftsman. So I may have considered his counsel as something I would want to know more about.

The seminar began at FAFC on a Friday evening. On Saturday, we met in groups. The day was split by a nice luncheon, and that afternoon Joe visited the group I was working with and asked if he could borrow me for a spell. He took me to an area off-stage and behind the organ in the main auditorium, where three members I knew welcomed me. After he left me with them, these members offered me a chair and gathered around me to lay their hands on my shoulders. Then they prayed over me, and some used their heavenly language. This experience reminded me of biblical accounts of the apostles performing what in my old church was called "holy sealing," also called the rebirth with the Holy Spirit, during which New Testament accounts of Pentecost report that the recipients responded by speaking in tongues as proof that the Holy Spirit had indeed visited them by way of that dispensation.

I really was not sure what to expect. But by the end of the prayers, I had experienced no inclinations to utter any words other than in my native tongue (English), nor was I told that a similar result might occur. I later shared my thoughts about the day's events with Joe, telling him that I had not felt any urge to speak in tongues. He suggested I take some time alone to contemplate and just become quiet within myself.

One morning the following week, I was home alone and followed Joe's suggestion. I sat in my favorite chair and focused on my breathing. I had practiced meditation before and began by silently relaxing each part of my body. When my mind wandered, I focused on each breath and the movement of my lungs as they filled and emptied, a practice to distract my mind and deny it any avenue of thought.

Time passed unnoticed. I was not sleepy. My eyes were closed, but I was not dreaming. Then, in my mind, I began to hear words not in any language I recognized. I could also see them in written form in my mind's eye. Not exactly sure what to expect, I captured those words in my memory as they stayed in my thoughts. I still did not have an urge to speak out loud. Then I got up and, still aware of what seemed to be a phrase, wrote it down on paper. The next thing that happened really freaked me out. I had never composed music before. But there in my mind, as those words remained present, I also heard a melody. Drawing five lines (the musical staff) on a piece of paper, I sat at the keyboard and plunked out the tune, then wrote the notes on the paper. Repeating the whole phrase several times, and still in a state of euphoria, I added harmony to the melody. Next, I added the lyrics, which were the words I had seen in my head and written down. Finally, I sang the song. A fair amount of time had passed and at each step

I kept wondering what was taking place. Whatever was happening, it had not ended yet. I knew what those words meant. I could interpret them. It was a song of praise. So I wrote down the English version. By this time, of course, I was feeling frightened and anxious, and I sat there at the piano for a while, feeling perplexed. Unsettling as this "revelation" was, I was not sure who to share this with. That evening, I told Beth, who had also come away from the weekend unmoved, about my experience. She had nothing to say and might have thought I'd lost it.

Was this what Joe meant by getting pulled in kicking and screaming?

I needed to think about how I was going to share this experience. When I called Joe Jenkins a few days later, he was, well...I'm not sure how to explain his reaction other than to use the word "incredulous." He and I were both thinking that my mind was playing some trick on me. "Bill," Joe told me, "I'm not sure that you were actually speaking a heavenly language. I've never heard of anything like this before." I can still hear his familiar twang in my head and his response. It left me hanging and, if I'm honest, dejected. I don't know what I had been expecting him to say.

The experience was hard to process and even harder to share with Joe. I finally decided to destroy the manuscript. To me, the matter was closed. I was not sure how this would reflect on me. When I called Joe (while reviewing this episode in my draft) to refresh my memory, he reassured me that there had been no obstacles that he could imagine that would have stood in my way should I have pursued the ministry in the Foursquare denomination. I will never forget the sequence of events, the clear text in my head, the melody, the notes, and the translation I created. I can imagine this same anomaly triggering the genesis of several churches throughout history. I had recently been a part of one such church.

Looking back again now, I believe it was my mind in a state of creativity that produced that extraordinary moment. I have always been creative and have often surprised myself when unique solutions made their way out of my subconscious and into the morning light. If I faced a challenge of any sort I'd tuck it away, bringing it to bed with me, and in the morning or during the next day a light would go on. But one thing I was sure of: it was not the Holy Spirit, not God, nor anything supernatural that I had experienced. It was a unique demonstration of what our untapped, magnificent human brain is capable of. I had presented my brain with a challenge, and my brain went über-creative and presented me with one hell of a solution. And while my brain apparently missed the mark regarding the particular definition of a heavenly language in (I assume) the eyes of the Foursquare faith, it had also provided me with an experience that both frightened me and left me aware of some powerful juju having nothing to do with the paranormal.

Setting aside what had happened, I began to concentrate on my classes and everyday life. I was still working freelance and could get quite busy. I was used to long days, and multitasking was just the way I had learned to roll.

***

My folks spoke German when they did not want *die Kinder* to understand what they were talking about. Except for maybe a greeting at church once in a while, I never heard my parents speak German at other times. *Geld* was money, and when they wanted to surprise us with an ice cream cone, my dad would ask my mom, "*Hast Du Geld?*" I had learned a few words here and there also while preparing for a trip to Germany to visit family in 1999.

Pleased that the Cerritos College offered German, I enrolled in German 101 in the summer and German 102 in the fall of 2007. For the time being,

I would stick to languages that could get me *ein Bier und eine Wurst* (a beer and a sausage). Also, I had never used algebra enough in my life to pass the math evaluation needed for graduation, and because I was unable to prove that I would never use algebra in my next life, I bowed to the rules and added Pre-Algebra that fall.

By the spring of 2008, I was on the home stretch to achieving my degree. I needed just three more classes to top off the credits for an AA. Another four units of algebra would take care of my math require-ments, which left me two elective choices. World Religions, with the same philosophy professor, and Philosophy of the Bible II: Christian Scripture would do nicely to satisfy these electives.

By this time my head was swimming with reconstituted doubts about all things Godly. Beth and I were still going to services and socializing in every niche we had carved out for ourselves at FAFC. My desire to re-enter the ministry, however, had cooled. It seemed like a great deal of time had passed since I'd been told there would be an invitation to take the polity course to qualify for ordination. This gap troubled me in some ways. But one day the call came. It took me by surprise. "Hey, Bill, I've got some fantastic news." Joe sounded excited. That much I remember. That and his dejected tone when he later asked me, "Well, what's happened?" Enough time had passed that I had confused ordination with the next step, which was the polity course. There was enough doubt in me at this point to decline the offer to enroll in the course on the spot. Joe sounded as confounded as I felt relieved. It was starting to feel like another watershed moment was about to happen in my life.

Meanwhile, I read an announcement soliciting students who were on a teaching track. I spoke with a counselor about what it would take to teach industrial arts and how much credit I could get, having worked in manufacturing my entire life. I left with a free backpack and little hope of using what I already knew to teach.

24

A Preponderance of Evidence

When the lights came back on

Returning to community college to finish my AA degree before entering the seminary, though I considered it a detour, was a blessing in disguise. Or the beat of a cosmic butterfly's wing, which, if you believe in the chaos theory, suggests that the smallest thing can initiate monumental change. More than once, I had wondered what continuing my education could have offered me had I chosen curiosity over dogma earlier in life. Back at school, now in my mid-fifties, I relished being challenged to think and then present my conclusions based on the subject matter at hand. The timing was perfect in that the courses I was taking addressed some nagging questions that I was tired of ignoring.

My first and last semesters at Cerritos College included four courses that considered cosmology from different aspects. Cosmology (not to be confused with cosmetology), regardless of which school of thought you promote, seeks to explain the provenance and future of the universe. From a secular point of view, both philosophy and astronomy (not to be confused with astrology) combine a collection of ideas and empirical information with which we can consider our origins and fate. But from a religious point of view, philosophy can ignore damning evidence that threatens Old Testament beliefs.

The school of thought I had, so to say, attended until now, depended on faith in a deity to answer all questions regarding the origins of the universe and mankind. Up to that point in my life, I had compartmentalized evidence of this kind—science in one drawer, religion in another—and believed it was best not to attempt reconciliation. Like oil and vinegar, they stubbornly remained apart. The "holy oil," demanding absolute faith, would not mix easily with the acidic scientific facts like Darwin's theory of evolution. The folks in my current denomination never placed both on the same table.

Huston Smith (1919–2016) was a world-renowned religious scholar and author of *The World's Religions*, the textbook used in my World Religions course. He was born in China, where his father was a Christian missionary, and he grew up believing as his parents did. During his post-graduate studies in the U.S., after he read Gerald Heard and Aldous Huxley, he began to inquire about mysticism, transcendentalism, and other belief systems. He finally came to embrace the Perennial Philosophy, whose goal is the commonality of all religions. Through his 1950s TV series and textbook, *The Religions of Man*, he became the celebrity and scholar we have come to know for his in-depth knowledge of the world's religions and his wise opinions on the subject.

I was first introduced to Smith through the PBS series, *Bill Moyers: The Wisdom of Faith with Huston Smith*. Smith was an impressive man, and I enjoyed the subject matter these two men discussed in depth.

It made sense that my professor, also a theist, would choose this scholar and his book to teach the course in world religions. In both courses, Philosophy 101 and World Religions, the same professor assigned journaling as part of the coursework; it was (and is) a sure way to sift through one's own ideas, both old and new. When I began writing this memoir, I referred to my handwritten pages from both classes.

I only learned recently that Smith's primary belief was based on the Perennial Philosophy. What he was interested in and pursued in his life was a metaphysical truth which defined the spiritual nature of our existence. His concept of the natural world and our universe is accurately described by what science can substantiate and is not based on religious texts. Throughout my own life of faith, I had considered the ultimate truth to be what I learned from my parents and the Church, my one major adjustment being my encounter with Alex Klein in my thirties.

For years, Christianity and its many denominations were the only belief systems that I spent time comparing. I would find it curious when one Christian high school football team prayed to God for victory over another. Were they asking God to choose a mere football team? And how did they live with the answer? What did victory in the game prove? On a deeper level, I naively questioned why the Spirit of God, who promised to lead us (I assumed he meant all Christians) into all truth, could not bring all denominations into a unified belief. *"Howbeit when he, the Spirit of truth, is come, he will guide you into all truth..."* (John 16:13 KJV).

The material in the World Religions class compared the similarities and differences of the beliefs of the major world religions: each religion motivated to understand the truth about the spiritual component to life. One of my key beliefs, and one that found its way into many of my sermons, was that we are all spiritual beings, and this life is just a brief moment (a parenthesis) we spend having a natural or human experience. After considering the world's major religions and witnessing the dedication of their adherents, I had to ask, what could one man possess that elevated his set of beliefs above another's? Sometimes people will die in deference to their choice of beliefs. How do we extract from these speculative and diverse approaches a single truth that explains everything? I can definitely see the advantage of believing that all religious beliefs originated from one truth, but good luck convincing most believers that their brand was *not* somehow superior to all others.

The only thing common to these major religions—Christianity, Islam, Buddhism, etc.—is the human mind, and for millennia, men have pondered variations of the same theme. "How did I get here and what should I do with my life? Oh, and how do I beat death?" That's a big one. One group applies their intuition excluding empirical evidence, another excludes religious concepts, and yet another tries to imagine a hybrid philosophy. As Smith maintained a belief in God until his passing, he placed science and philosophy in lesser roles while defining his ultimate reality. Religion remained the priority within his own consciousness, which he placed above empirical evidence, which was what man could hold in his hand, see with his eyes, measure with his tools, and otherwise consider a part of the physical world. While Smith preferred Christianity, he did not dismiss knowledge of science or the avenues of inquiry made by other religions, which he also practiced. However, he chose the comfort of his original upbringing in Christianity and especially its concept of forgiveness. He preferred the conclusions that his own consciousness had provided.

It was becoming clear to me that I needed to arrive at some conclusions of my own. I was also coming to see that this all-important personal peace was what I had been wrestling with for my entire life. I was back at those cold concrete steps in junior high, but this time I had considerably more evidence to make use of in my deliberations. That which Alex Klein had taught me so adeptly by presenting the knowledge of the Gospel was just the beginning. I was now learning to compare and to question all knowledge. The personal beliefs that I had accumulated over my lifetime were now in the company of several other ideas, or ways to look at the big picture. There was one clear similarity. That collection of human wisdom which entire populations were dedicated to upholding was basically a product of human thought regarding the big questions of human existence, each one rising out of humanity's propensity to imagine, conjure, compare, evaluate, and investigate. And all of those concepts were susceptible to humanity's inherent flaws: our ego, our hubris, our need to be accepted, and our need to be worshipped.

The information I was using to define my own world was growing and evolving, and to see this new cosmological mural would require that I continue stepping back as I considered and selected which ideas best defined my new Truth.

While I was considering the ideas of the ages regarding how we had come to be and how to assign meaning to our lives, I was also getting an earful, as my other philosophy professor was laying out the provenance of the New Testament and the Christian philosophy it presented. An obvious pattern of missing links was coming into play regarding the authenticity of the life of Christ. The gap between his death and a readable New Testament, based on the dubious materials available, seemed more like a game of pin the tail on the donkey than a scholarly assembly of historically accurate information.

I learned that storytelling was the mode of communication which brought the New Testament into existence. By the time someone started writing down these stories, centuries had passed, and the cast of characters were all deceased. The Bible makes quite a thud on the floor when it falls from a minister's toolbox.

Hollywood has suggested that the story of Jesus was "the greatest story ever told." Aside from considering the lives lived, and lost, in promoting Christianity over its two thousand years of history, I could not ignore my own creative mind as it sketched out scenarios about how the New Testament came to exist. The first point of view I took was to consider my own proclivities related to human nature. It is hard for people to resist the temptation to place their interests over another's. There are many reasons why humans and organizations might manipulate a story. The need to validate and collect hearsay and record it for posterity and/or for potential profit or to persuade the meek, suggest to me that such a story could have been easily modified to fit various agendas.

Alex Klein convinced me that Jesus was a loving teacher, a man filled with grace and understanding. So how does the following story, which takes place after his ascension, make sense? St. Peter called out a man named Ananias, and later that day, his wife Sapphira, because they had conspired to hold back part of the profits from the sale of their property. (At the time Christians sold all they had, the whole being held by the Church in common.) Peter accused the man of lying to the Holy Spirit, and the result was that the husband dropped dead. Then, later, when the wife also lied, she dropped dead too (Acts 5:1-11).

Was this what Jesus would have done?

***

While school was challenging my beliefs, I had to be careful not to introduce any of my musings into the rhetoric I might employ at church, whether in a classroom or in private discussions. It would be like grabbing someone cozily huddled near a fireplace and shoving them out into a frozen lake.

Beth and I invited a group of church friends to our home for a New Year's Eve party. We played a few party games, and the game I was most curious about has a couple of names: "Chinese whispers" and "the telephone game." Although I did not dare make a comparison, I wondered if anyone in our circle might someday stop and think, "I wonder if this is how the Bible came into being." If you don't remember the gist of the game, participant number one reads a sentence or phrase to themself, then whispers this sentence or phrase into the ear of the person sitting next to them, and so it goes around the circle. The last person in the circle speaks aloud what they heard. The difference between the original and final phrase can be astonishing. (I wonder if a lawyer has ever tried this with a jury.) A message can be diluted or tweaked by circumstance, a distraction, a triggered memory, or a glance from across the room and—voilà, the original phrase takes on a life of its own.

What transpired over the roughly three hundred years between the last disciple's death and the creation of the first Canon? Various scholars have their opinions, I have mine. Even with a version of the New Testament that can easily be read in modern English, there remain questions about how to interpret the material. How does one deal with conflicting reports, such as the episode I recounted above? What difference does it make if you read the Greek, Aramaic, or Latin manuscripts? Does language increase your chances of understanding the thousandth iteration of a verse that began two thousand years ago as a whisper or a shout? To suggest that the Bible be taken literally leaves one holding the parts of a thousand-year-old puzzle that can never be assembled into anything resembling a single "Truth."

And yet I wanted, if not needed, to *believe*. I continued my pursuit, my meager faith elbowing aside the other beliefs in the lineup while my hope kept grasping at the memories of my youth and my feelings of euphoria when I was entranced by the sermons of Alex Klein.

At Florence Avenue, I thrived for a while as I nurtured my joy and my faith. But, like a block of ice with a hot ice pick stuck deep into it, tiny cracks began to form in my belief system. I realized this new information percolating in my mind was no small thing. I wrote the following as a journal entry for my class in World Religions. (It's unedited, written before class, a stream of consciousness.)

***

Feeling—*I spent seven minutes considering what I'm currently feeling. Still no definitive adjective forthcoming. Yesterday I went to church and could not get much, if anything, from the service/sermon. After church, we took a bike ride to a few parks, during which or at which I read the text on Confucius (Smith). This was worthwhile. I can relate to his (Confucius') one-world-at-a-time concept regarding the afterlife. Body and soul and spirit, yes, but at the present human. Why not get the most out of it? I can appreciate his view of the arts-I thrive on beauty-physical, architectural, musical, artistic.* [March 3, 2008, 9:33 A.M. Campus Library. Emphasis added].

***

The three philosophy courses I took in college presented two millennia of opinions on what the mind of man can come up with regarding the big questions. Where did we come from? What purpose were our lives meant to serve? For centuries, we looked heavenward, some of us believing the world was flat, although when I look at the moon I see a sphere. Nevertheless, yes, there was no perspective other than one's own "backyard." But one course, Astrobiology (our professor's class description) or Astronomy 104, transported me back in time, way past that flat earth mindset. While those ancient philosophers made use of the same evolved brain as I and those in my classroom used, they did not have the accumulated knowledge that we had at our fingertips in this class setting. Our professor was not presenting supposition or information provided by a prophet claiming that God had told him how He had created him and his neighbors. The information we discussed in class was factual, observable, and defined by scientific principles using mathematics, chemistry, biology, and physics. The astronomer teaching the class presented 13.8 billion years of history using an array of modern telescopes. She explained, with precision, how we came to be where we stand as *Homo sapiens*, but not why.

To a believer maintaining a particular set of ideas on Genesis and the afterlife, it is quite an eye opener when you're presented with that much empirical knowledge offering such a clear explanation. My Genesis story was based on a collection of stories written by men who supposedly recorded about 6,000 years of history, which, when combined, suggested "the truth with a "big T' regarding our existence. Also, that information was provided by a supernatural God who, the same men said, inspired their thoughts. How else would they be able to report the details of their own creation or the conditions prior to that initial event? Do you see the problem? Their idea about God was inspired by God, and sometimes, they could hear His voice. Or was that an ass speaking[1]?

It was time to wake up. Just like those moments when you first stir from dreams, there comes a point where you tell yourself, "Now. Now open those eyes. Sit up and consider the new day. Take a deep breath and accept that you are a living, thinking being." I could no longer just accept the old status quo. The new information I was learning needed my full attention. I owed it to myself to acknowledge my naiveté.

---

1. The donkey said to Balaam, "Am I not your own donkey, which you have always ridden, to this day? Have I been in the habit of doing this to you?" Numbers 22:30 NIV

It was time, for me anyway, to update my place in the grand scheme of things. Humans had ascended in matters of science and technology, and it was time for me to acknowledge the new information relative to a selection of still inconclusive answers. The questions had not changed, but the lab in which I could suss out the answers surely had.

25
Who Would Jesus Vote For?

Hello, excuse me, can you tell me how I can get an absentee ballot for my friend?

When Terry Risser described his congregation as conservative, it did not occur to me that he was stating a political persuasion. The concept of politics and religion sharing a bed was something I could not relate to. I had considered that matter settled by the official separation of church and state in the United States. The politics of our nation had never affected me in my old Platonic cave (the NAC), but as early as November 2006, there were rumblings at Florence Avenue about the loss of both houses to the Democrats in the midterm elections. In 2008, the presidency was up for grabs. The Democrat chosen by his party would become the first black President of the United States: Barack Obama.

Beth and I first noticed the dissonance from a few individuals in our adult Sunday School group. She and I were both politically center left. I voted for the man or the woman, not the party. I was not into the grassroots pushing and shoving that I was being introduced to. Those with conservative views were well represented at FAFC however, and they were becoming more and more vociferous. Beth and I focused on our faith and our friends. We avoided political discussions. When one church member decided to run for office after the shake-up in Washington, D.C., several members laid hands on him as part of a service and prayed for his success. This was an endorsement and the most overt gesture involving the whole congregation that we had witnessed so far. But Beth and I could handle most of the lid banging. Most of our friends did not dwell on those matters.

When Barack Obama laid his hand on the Bible to take his oath of office, there was little joy in our church. If Colin Powell had run and won, horns would be blaring. But Powell missed his chance. In fact, I might have voted for the man. I remember wishing he would have run instead of G. W. Bush. But now the White House had a Democrat at the helm and—Lord help us—. Beth and I would do our best to accommodate the drum beating. For the next two years we shrugged off the occasional, sometimes blatant, but mostly muted, undercurrents.

Time had passed, and two things had become clear. My decision not to pursue the ministry, combined with my deliberations on a belief system in crisis, was creating a personal dilemma in my life. The whispered declarations about the nation's politics continued to make us uneasy. As 2010 wound down, we agreed: come the New Year, we would turn the page and start looking for a new church.

In January 2011, as we made good on our plan, the list of potential churches we started with became shorter each Sunday. Each visit left us feeling blasé. If it had just been me, I might have considered the fact that I was now dealing with a raging set of doubts and that I was in denial about those doubts and hoping they would go away on their own. But Beth was not feeling any love for the new churches either, as we slipped in and out of several local congregations.

Back in September 2010, my sister had called to let me know Dad had had an episode at home. That event signaled that Alzheimer's was proving predictable. It had been almost eight years since the initial diagnosis. This time span marked when the average patient succumbed to the disease.

As we were setting out in a new direction, Dad had already gone 'round the corner and no longer recognized us or trusted Mom, which broke her heart. The next few months would be quite challenging. My mom had been attending a support group for caregivers that was critical to her well-being. She had cared for the love of her life alone from the start and had awakened to the same love each day, not tracking the minute changes day by day. We only visited a few times a year, and when we did, it felt like a moment of free fall after miscalculating the next step down. Mom finally had no choice but to learn how to live alone with a man who could no longer recognize her. There was outside help to watch him when she went to church or went shopping. Although a musical therapist, guitar in hand, sang for Dad, taming the beast within, his world was confusing and threatening. During the incident in September, he had become violent, and the police had been called. They had taken him to the ER for evaluation. Dad did not harm Mom, but he left her very frightened. She would still insist on continuing his care, but there would be a different approach to his illness and closer monitoring. Early in February 2011, Dad's condition worsened. We suspended our hunt for churches. I packed my bags for Boise.

Even an ostrich must come up for air, food, or to peck at an itch. It's amazing what us humans force ourselves to believe when faced with adversity. I sat at the kitchen table in my parents' home, still pretending my dad was at the table with me, but he had departed a while ago, the disease suspending him just out of reach of our world. Mom and Dad had lovingly nested here after he had retired from the ministry almost fifteen years earlier. Their cozy two-bedroom home, once listed in a Sears & Roebuck catalog, had been a kit which the original owner had purchased and assembled atop a thick-walled foundation that covered a small musty basement, probably called a root cellar back in the day. Its charm had housed a lifetime of joy and sorrow, and now this cherished stage was the set for my father's last days.

Mom and Dad had designed and maintained a masterful garden in their backyard. It was a work of love, with Dad constantly trying to buy more vegetables and fruit trees than they had room for. But as his disease progressed, Mom was forced to get inventive to keep him safe. For example, the time I made a trip to Boise to take his pickup truck home with me, Mom had convinced him to give the truck to me for my construction business. This pleased him greatly. I still park it in front of my home, today it's our second car. He was so proud of their garden, always adding plants to the cart at the nursery, my mom always making up reasons to put them back. One day, he brought in a snake he'd just killed with the pruning shears. My mom smiled on the outside, but cried on the inside at the sight of a section of garden hose he proudly held. The time they'd spent living in, and caring for, that home and garden was now dwarfed by the years that he'd spent in decline.

During that visit in 2011, we had plenty of time to reminisce with Mom about their life. Hours passed while I hoped Dad would make an appearance, even though I knew he could not recognize me as his son. His doctor had prescribed medications to calm his mind. I saw an exercise toy on the table. "Wanna play catch, Dad?" I pushed his wheelchair back from the table and faced him in my chair. We were just a few feet from each other. I tossed the star-shaped toy into his lap. He surprised me and caught it. Breaking into a smile, he tossed it back, his tongue peeking out between his lips, a signature expression whenever he attempted to focus on a task. His smile remained as I caught it, too. We got three or four tosses in before he left again. For a fleeting moment, we had connected as a father and son might, although how his brain had framed the moment, who knows? Dad had played on his high school's varsity baseball team as a catcher, not my position of choice. Too dangerous. But no sooner had we shared those few tosses than a dark shadow distracted him, and away he disappeared into the fog again. That is the last memory I have of him in a semi-alert state. There is no telling how his mind made sense of his surroundings, or the way he framed his life. It must have been like doing several different puzzles, the ones where no picture is provided. There's no way to know whether the memories we shared with him helped him remember the joys we once shared, or just slipped off the edge of the table forever lost.

With his physician's advice, we had agreed to withhold treatment for Dad's chronic urinary tract infections. Now he was in hospice care, and his suffering would soon be over. For the next month and a half, I made several open-ticketed trips to Boise. On Pi Day, March 14, 2011, Dad finally found rest from that miserable disease. He would no longer fear the strangers in his house who loved him. The eyes of the dead do not stay closed on their own; however, I lend him mine whenever I see those that we both loved and those he would never meet. Part of the DNA he passed on to me is still present as I hug my grandchildren.

Considering the number of patients who suffer the ravages of Alzheimer's, it is a travesty that the laws which allow one to take their own life in the face of a fatal disease in some states do not exist in other states. Why rob people of their dignity in their last months of life? Lawmakers need to find a way so that people still capable of thinking on their own can plan their departure and thus have a final say in their last moments. Such a law when my dad was ill could have spared us all a great deal of unnecessary suffering, and most especially him.

26

Souls Set Free

Shopping for rafters

"Hey, Bill, Terry Risser here. Say, we've missed you guys." It had been two weeks since my dad had passed and four months since we had attended a service at Foursquare. I was expecting Terry's call. I'd been overwhelmed by my life, and after Dad had passed, was still in denial about my faith, so I wasn't sure how to explain our absence. Since January 2011, Beth and I had visited at least a half dozen churches, plus I had spent most of February and March, including the last three weeks of my dad's life, in Boise. So I had been expecting a call for some time already.

"How are you and Beth doing?" Terry asked. That was a tough question. I shared the two most important pieces of information he needed to know at the moment: my dad's passing and the reality that I was having a crisis of faith. These two points had nothing to do with each other, though I imagined him thinking one had triggered the other and pushed me over the cliff. He offered his condolences. He hadn't been expecting to hear about my dad, and I'm sure he offered his help if I needed to talk. After we said goodbye, I took some time to say what I had not had the words for during our call. I wanted to have said more than I did and needed time to figure out how to let him down as easily as I could. The following email is my considered response to my friend. It is unedited here.

***

Dear Pastor Terry,

I appreciate your call this morning. I wanted to have a "wider" conversation with you. However, it did not seem to be the right moment. While it has been a challenging time since September when my dad took a turn for the worse, I have also been struggling with my personal faith for some time now. I have had a few intimate conversations with Dorothy. Beth and I had been attending her Sunday school class up until the first of this year.

When we first came to FAFC, I was quite frank about my "progressive" outlook regarding Christianity. You were equally honest in describing FAFC as a conservative Christian church.

Beth and I felt very much at home and very welcome in the congregation. We always find the sermons helpful and spirit led. The challenge for us has been finding friends we can "let our hair down with," Even though the pastors have been very understanding and tolerant of my ideas, (which I suppose as pastors we ought to be, everyone is entitled to their own specific beliefs) we seem to find though that our relationships, once begun, plateau and then fade when we share our honest feelings. Mostly, it becomes evident that some of my ideas would not be welcomed either way.

I, in particular, have been in need of some frank conversation regarding my beliefs. Unfortunately, even though I'm positive you or any of the pastors at FAFC would be willing to engage with me, I know, because of the fundamental beliefs, I would be placing most in a difficult position.

We have been procrastinating about looking for a church home that might be more flexible to our liberal tendencies. We have no complaints about FAFC it was (and in many ways still is) a Bethany for us.

I'm not sure what the future will hold for us. We will always have good things to say about Florence Avenue and, I'm not sure this is good-bye either, we'll have to see...

With great appreciation,

Beth and I were enjoying our Sundays off and, after visiting a hodge-podge of congregations earlier in the year, had decided to just take a break. For the time being, we would end our search, each of us pursuing our own spiritual connection. I considered a home church, which I had often thought would be easier to model after the first Christian church.

The problem here was the conflicting thoughts I brought to the table any time I considered my options. I had this nagging need to somehow resuscitate my faith, so I often searched online for a liberal version of the Church, or at least a neutral version. My new reality existed in one part of my brain at this point. There I had a clear cosmology sketched out, one based on scientific evidence and the mythical nature of the Bible. I was determined to do everything I could to salvage some part of that idealistic world I'd grown up in.

Could it be that the human tendency to lean into a cure, the placebo effect, is what believing in God is all about? We all know that there's no way some carpenter, laden with hammer and nails and a giant board on his shoulder, could have walked on water. And that his old man had created the multiverse? Preposterous!

When I found Greg Boyd on a podcast, I wanted to believe again. I thought this guy might do the trick. Christianity was my safe place, even though the walls were losing their insulation and the sun was shining through the roof.

Theologian and apologist Dr. Gregory Boyd of Woodland Hills Church in St. Paul, Minnesota, addressed some of my key issues. He had found a compromise between science and faith and is a brilliant apologist. After I listened to a few of his sermons, I invited Beth to join me as a "podrisioner." (This is Greg's play on the words "podcast" and "parishioner," a name he assigned to those that joined his congregation online.) My wife and I sat in our living room as if we had a front-row seat in his church. I was hoping he could lift me back on my tricycle. The reality, which I ignored like a gentle knock at my door, was just working its way past six decades of sacred conditioning. I needed time to accept my conclusions and abandon the idea of keeping one foot in my safe place.

The Easter after my dad passed, we attended our first sunrise service at a church about thirty-five minutes from our house. Paz Naz was a large Nazarene church in Pasadena that had an outstanding music program. The sounds of a large, conventional choir with a matching orchestra warmed me like a hit of schnapps (perhaps suggesting I had a dependency problem). I came for the donuts and the friendship, plus eating out after the service with friends. My secret friend, Jesus? Him, I ghosted. I now considered his teachings ancient wisdom, and only associated with a historical figure (not the son of God) who'd made quite a splash, but who no longer answered his texts.

Some longtime friends, family by marriage who had also left the NAC, had been singing Paz Naz's praises, and we'd gotten curious. We dropped in about once a month to start and then increased our visits. We were both managing our expectations, though, and were wary of getting too involved. The distance from home made it easy to just be Sunday visitors. It was enough to satisfy our needs. I would stay, so to speak, sober for a few weeks before needing to come around for a shot.

Greg Boyd's podcast was still in the mix, too, and I read his book, *Letters From a Skeptic: A Son Wrestles with His Father's Questions about Christianity*,[1] which is a collection of letters he had exchanged with his skeptic father. I was back to analyzing my choices, and secularism was winning. I was not being persuaded, as Greg's father had been, about the reliability

---

1. Published by David C. Cook, 1994.

of a belief based on a dubious collection of old manuscripts. That and the reliability of human recollection. Men had fabricated some powerful and absolute dogmas over the years. The claim that the Holy Spirit was guiding the process? That I could debunk with my eyes closed.

There were two clear aspects to the life we now had in the Church: (1) the supernatural belief system and (2) the close human bonds we had established within it.

A decade later, I'd make a new friend who found his solution in a small group that he and his wife belong to. He still finds comfort in the New Testament by stripping it of any supernatural overtones. It's similar to Thomas Jefferson's take on Jesus' life. Jefferson assembled a book called *The Life and Morals of Jesus of Nazareth,*[2] in which he created a picture of the life of Jesus without the miracles. My friend maintains a fellowship with similar thinking friends.

Even hearing about what he holds onto today, I'm not sure it's something I need anymore. Friendships, yes, but nothing that refers back to the life of Jesus. Instead, I have found comfort among a group of ex-ministers who meet mostly online and share a common bond. We support each other as members of the Clergy Project. That's where I met this new friend.

Another source of comradery I've found just in recent months is writing for Medium.[3] Here I have found a mutual admiration society based on our common talents, interests, and circumstances.

---

2. Jefferson cut and pasted the original copy for personal use. It was originally published as a lithographic reproduction in 1904 by the United States Government Printing Office in Washington D.C.

3. Wm Raff – Medium

But I would not find those two harbors for more than a decade after admitting I was an atheist.

By the start of 2012, Beth and I had ended all connections with organized religion. I had declared myself an atheist and begun pondering life as such. While I had yet to use the word in a sentence, written or out loud, I was finding it a clear marker defining the path I was on now, a point of demarcation. I walked on. Friends and family asked, "What's new?" I'd answer, "Everything and nothing."

Once again, that familiar line in the hymn "Amazing Grace" rang true: "I once was lost, but now am found, was blind, but now I see." After these lyrics became a point of reference when Alex Klein opened my eyes to the true teaching of Christ, now, like a double-edged sword, they swung again as an ironic truth.

But there was something weighing on me that was not quite in my line of vision. I noticed it every so often. Because it had been so recent, it made sense that my dad's death might be the cause. His passing did not feel the same to me as when my brother was killed. Dad's death freed him from the curse of Alzheimer's.

I struggled to put my finger on this silent visitor. Was it like an ocean current bringing up a chill from the deep? Or was it a shark passing near to its prey, sizing it up? Whatever it was, it remained out of reach for some time. I ruled out depression. I saw a counselor who made the same suggestion, but this feeling differed from my last bout with that long shadow.

When the curtain slowly opened, a great mural presented itself to me. Part hieroglyph, part interpretive relief, it seemed to rise like a great monolith in the desert. Before my eyes lay the ruins of a life of dedication, of friendships, sacrifice, investments, of expectations, untold joy, and sadness. There was even an imprint of my time invested in our last church, which I had also once had great hopes for. But an investment in Heaven was now made worthless by a greater truth.

Like one of the Voyager space probes, I was free of the gravity of religion. I watched as that old life, spinning on its own axis, appeared frozen in time. It had once been the only world I knew, but now it faded as I traveled further and further away. And, like Voyager, I wondered how much time I had left in my power supply. Was there enough reserve to fuel my next chapter? What could I contribute to the world with what time I had left? What to do in my new role as an atheist?

Even though my earlier life had been powered by what now seemed insignificant, relative to my new reality, it still offered a rich tapestry of fond memories. I had burned most of my allotted candle in that make-believe world, and now I was not happy about the missed opportunities, especially the ones dependent on youth. But once I took that all in, once I made peace with it all, I realized that if I'd left something undone...well, it was too late now. And that was okay. When I studied and absorbed that grand body of work, when I acknowledged its historical significance, I tipped my hat to it and went on my way. But I still pause to turn back. The joy is close. The disappointment, where I left it, is not worth the effort to dwell on.

If anything, this book is an attempt to capture that life in the form of an expansive mural, so to speak. I hope I've conveyed the significance of my journey as it pertains to who I was and now am. The part I took with me, the most important part, remains. I'm right here if you want to visit.

I remember standing on a landing outside the NAC church in Anaheim before I retired. Leonard Kolb Jr. approached me. We shook hands. I asked him if he understood why I was retiring. He nodded or said yes (I'm not sure anymore). Then he added, "You probably won't be the last."

Part Three

My New Life

27

Helping Others Understand

It's not you, it's me…

After Dad passed, my sister and I proposed to Mom that she might like to live seasonally with us. That is, she could summer in Idaho and winter in Southern California. She loved the idea. I think she had a plan in her back pocket, knowing the day would come when she would have to sell their home. Mom and Dad had fallen in love with it when they retired to Boise, but now the garden they had created was too grand for one person to care for and it had suffered through Dad's final years. Some generous friends who had recently befriended Mom volunteered to make some repairs to the house and help get everything in tiptop shape. It sold fast.

When Mom arrived for her first extended stay with Beth and me, almost a year had passed since we had stepped foot into any church for a religious reason. Mom knew something about our situation but did not know how far I had moved along on my journey away from faith. I approached her for a serious heart-to-heart talk after breakfast one morning, feeling like a parent needing to preface our conversation with, "This is going to hurt me more than it hurts you." However, the opposite was more accurate because there was no easy way to tell her that I had no interest whatsoever in attending a church again and there was no room in my heart or my head for a deity. By this time, I had clear-cut every mythical idea she had ever planted and nurtured in my soul back when I was a child. I now considered myself an atheist, though I had not yet spoken the word out loud in a sentence.

"You know, Mom, that we've stopped going to church." I began at the shallow end of the pool and watched as her posture revealed her disappointment. Then I said we no longer prayed to bless the food at mealtime, either. Mom was not one to become belligerent or sob and weep. Instead, she steeled herself, a trait she had inherited from her own mother, to prepare her soul for sorrow, but also for battle. Her spiritual defense mechanism alerted her that there was a threat facing her. She braced herself for bad news, as if she was about to hear she'd lost another son.

I had heard the cautionary tale many times in NAC sermons in the past, the story about the unfaithful son whose decision killed his mother as he turned his back on the faith she had sown into his unborn seed, a death which brought him back to church for her funeral. That, and a dozen more cleverly crafted tales, had left their marks and now wriggled under my skin, whether I was an atheist or not.

"But you still believe in God, don't you?" she asked me. "I don't believe I do," was my answer. My mind flashed back to the mothers who had presented their crushed souls to me when I was a minister. "Please pray for my child." "Could you have a chat with him or her?" "He was such a faithful little man and enjoyed Sunday School so much." But I could not help them. I'd witnessed every Christmas and Easter as those grown children had acquiesced, satisfying a mother's plea, their reluctant attendance producing some fleeting hope, as if this one venture back into the hallowed venue could reignite their faith. This all clicked in my mind like an old theater projector, and I saw the flickering images of divided families bound by the primordial bond of life, the empty nest, the cycle complete but not comprehended by the parent.

I continued to make my case with my own mom. "I could never lie to you about this," I told her. "Mom, I know you and what your faith means to you. If I could flip a switch to avoid hurting you, I would, but I can't lie to myself, either. The only way I can move forward is to open myself to you and not hide my reality."

I was fortunate. I know people who had cut all ties with family members who left the Church. Some who left were denied their inheritance because they refused to repent. But my mother would move Heaven with her prayers before threatening harm to any of her children. Putting myself in her shoes, I knew my name would always be on her lips when she approached God's throne; I imagined her hand hovering over the offering box on the high holy days, reminding Him of the lost soul she would always love. I smiled when she promised to continue praying for me, knowing that her hope would prevail even though mine no longer did.

From that day forward, Mom would pray silently at every meal, and I would always love her and respect her faith. But even when she would come home from Church and report on the changes taking place, I could not respond in the way she hoped. She never accepted that I no longer believed in God and that alone meant that change, no matter how significant would not bring me back. I was glad the Church had softened its attitude toward other Christian faiths, that it had established charitable organizations to help anyone in need. It certainly appeared to me that the NAC, worldwide, had undergone a makeover that allowed them to coexist with the other Christian denominations with whom they shared the same savior and promised salvation. The most recent and remarkable change (I mentioned this earlier) was the acceptance of women into the ministry. Mom's bursts of hope, based on these changes, reminded me how much hope still lived in her soul and how far I had moved away from all things Christian.

My mother and other family members were the only people still in my life that I proactively shared my atheism with. In family gatherings, I shared my metamorphosis with anyone I knew would not take offense. I would not hide my perspective if, in a private conversation, someone mistakenly assumed my beliefs remained as they remembered them. I still wonder today if some people just refused to accept me and my new reality, or if they actually did not know where I hung my hat on the matter. Given the opportunity, I have no reservations about sharing my atheism with anyone, but I don't feel an imperative to force my beliefs on anyone, either. As long as we are all free to choose, and no one person or authority is demanding otherwise, I will not push any rocks up any hills. My life is too short for that. A decade or more has passed since I accepted my new reality in earnest, and it has become apparent to me, just over the last year, that some people are still unaware that I no longer believe in God and that they may learn about it for the first time here in this book.

***

Tim, an old friend from Florence Avenue, called me one day. "I miss you, Bill. Could we have lunch?" Honestly, while I missed many friends from both of the Churches which had been part of my life, I knew some people might consider my atheism as they would kryptonite. "Sure," I replied, "I'd love to." At the burger joint, once we had our food and the moment of truth arrived, I shared my new reality with Tim, the reality that I thought would matter the most going forward. Tim took a bite, nodding his head to indicate he was listening. "I just thought," I said, "I should put it on the table to start with." He said he didn't see a problem, adding it was brave of me to share that information.

The next time we met, it was soon clear that we had covered it all, we were all caught up as of that prior meeting. There was an awkwardness as we ate our last lunch together. "I didn't realize we would have so little to talk about," Tim said. These were his last words to me. I understood then and still do. That's just part of my new reality.

Talking about my atheism was much easier in my dentist's office, our conversations being fragmented over the extended silence of two cleanings six months apart. "How have you been, Bill?" "Pretty good. Fantastic, in fact! After a lifetime in the church and ministry, I now consider myself an atheist." Twenty minutes later, at the end of the polishing and a splash of mouthwash, the dentist asked, "What about life after death?" I would have loved to be present in her mind as the cleaning progressed and she deliberated over the information I had shared. But that was the end of the conversation that day. I grabbed some free travel-size dental goodies and made my next appointment. Unlike most small talk she may have been used to, I felt my announcement had left an impression. At our next appointment, she surprised me during a pause in the process and commented that, although she had been raised in a particular church herself, she had not been active for some time. We never broached the subject again.

As I write this book, it has become clear to me that many people do their best to avoid discussing religion. I suppose they've eked by in life and do not want others to know the extent of their convictions, or lack thereof. I can see why. Who wants to spring a trap by announcing amid those inclined to piety that they are non-believers? Most folks are shy and not ready to defend their beliefs. Some are even fearful to look either the doubter or the zealot in the eye. And then you have the guy on a corner not a half mile from my home who set up a string of shopping carts proclaiming his end-of-days theories. There was nothing subtle about his position.

Let's go back once more to those cold steps at my junior high. I decided then that I would be a willing voice regarding my beliefs. I had honed and polished my Christian testimony out of necessity because as a teenager I often proselytized door to door. I know...don't you just love it when some kid knocks on your door to tell you how great his church is? After Alex Klein rewrote that kind of testimony for me, I finally had a story I enjoyed sharing and did so with those who wanted to hear it. But now, after living in both worlds, I feel I have an even better story to tell, but I no longer need to share it with anyone other than those who share my curiosity and my point of view.

After years of rolling the term *atheist* around in my head and trying it out on this one or that one, I finally decided I needed to be prepared to better explain my position. If it's not a belief system we're talking about, then what is it?

28

Yep, I'm an Atheist

I'm as surprised as you are

Atheism beckoned at first like a grand wilderness inviting me to explore it. It did not offer structure or shelter. It felt to me like the Montana of philosophies, Big Sky Country. Its social fabric was too diverse for me to find a clear niche or a new place to lay my head. In my old world, the word "atheist" was a common noun like "angler" or "minister." In my new world, the word added several layers to my new reality, carrying with it two diverse implications. I would have preferred its basic meaning: I did not believe in any gods. I knew better, though, having had my own bias as a believer. So I joined an atheist group online and engaged with others who had no use for religion. Some had grown up without a god, whereas others had, like me, left a religious past. Religion had injured some. Escaping religion had left their families crushed, unwilling to forgive. For some of these individuals, it was like stepping out into oncoming traffic. They had not prepared themselves for the repercussions and had no point of reference without that old familiar support system, now behind them. They were looking for shelter and sympathy and thought if they posted memes criticizing the system that had broken them, it would somehow serve their cause. And, yeah, they'd found a group of equally disenfranchised souls, but what they did not realize was that they had joined a group of and for atheists and they were preaching to the choir.

Atheism, taken to mean anything more than just a label, presents too broad a spectrum for most people to comprehend in one glance. I needed to ponder its wares, take an inventory of what I considered sound and verifiable, and find out what, if anything, was worthy of my empty bookshelves. What kind of atheist did I want to be? An angry one? That would, I knew, be a waste of time. Perhaps I should do penance, seeking forgiveness from those I'd misled? Another waste of time. I imagined that most of my former associates were still thanking me for leaving quietly, or some version of that. Others in our situation were still pinching themselves to see if it was real or a dream.

One thing I had become sure of was that I was better off with the truth than living a lie. I think Beth and I both realized that we each needed to work out our own feelings regarding the changes we had made in our lives. Those changes were significant. We would need time to come to our own conclusions, time to define our new philosophies.

When my dad passed, I was not sure how I would feel or how I would mourn him. A long debilitating sickness like his Alzheimer's takes away pieces of your loved one, bit by bit. It's the cruelest part of Alzheimer's. I may have dealt with most of my mourning by the time he passed, feeling thankful that he no longer suffered, thankful that my mom could carry on by not being reminded daily of the lingering loss. He took a lot of her with him as he slowly disappeared. Today, he has only grown dearer to me as I spar with the nuances of what we shared, and both struggled to subdue as men. He subtly appears to me when I notice how our grandchildren's tongues peek out when concentrating or a smile telegraphs his presence across their happy faces, reminding me how our lineage remains connected over the ages. I am frequently amazed how such markers are, like breadcrumbs, scattered for my amusement when our grandchildren—his great grandchildren—are nearby.

It was shortly after he passed when I came to realize that I was also mourning my faith. In that five letter "F word," I enshrine a lifetime of commitment, significant time and treasure invested. The culture of a religious belief, of Christianity, is no small thing. I had a vested interest in its history, in the history of my denomination, in a family heritage representing the sacrifices of three generations. But was it all for naught? Was there nothing remaining? I've heard it said of a handful of others: "He threw it all away." Is that true of me, too? I would have argued that I'd exchanged it for greater treasure.

The years passed, the sting eased, reflection and calm came to rest between my new self and the diminishing regrets that signaled the end of mourning. I thought I had laid my old beliefs to rest, buried them under enough dirt that, I told myself, they had turned to dust by now. No need to dig anything up. Fine.

Then I came up with the idea of writing this memoir, and so shovels, so to speak, were purchased, gloves sized, courage summoned, and reasons contrived.

A life of that proportion begged for a grander funeral. And, dammit, I was going to give it one. I would invite everyone and, like Tom Sawyer and Huck Finn, observe from the balcony as the mourners filed past the coffin, salty eyed, giving a final f*#k-off and adieu.

The process of writing this memoir required an inventory of sorts. I had to re-collect everything I had thrown away. I had been warned that a memoir is not the place to air out grievances. For so many years, I had considered the matter of my former religious faith closed. I had forgiven everyone who'd had a hand in the godly deception. Forgiving myself primarily, now I waded in. And then I stopped, emotionally slammed, asking myself, should I get some therapy before continuing? I let time go by. What would I tell a person if they sat on my imaginary couch presenting the same lamentations I had? In my imagination, I sat in my old therapist Geoff's chair and asked myself, back on the couch, what I thought. "I think it would be best if you wrote it all down," my therapist-self told me. "Hang up the old feather bed and beat the shit out of it!" Ahh, back to anger management.

Damn! I gave it some more time.

During this past year, while continuing my DIY education to become an author, I read that most first novels are covertly autobiographical. Part of my education included a November of daily writing inspired by NaNoWriMo, or National Novel Writing Month. I stumbled on this in August 2021, a discovery that coincided with a Technicolor dream that snuck into my conscious world just as I woke up one morning. I was gifted with the vision of an illustrious world where trees the height of Mount Everest soared above the clouds. The creative juices poured out, turning into copious notes as I scrambled to learn how to outline, write, and create a novel from scratch. The result was a sci-fi fantasy with the working title *To Be or Not to Be*, which is yet to be published or even edited.

When I revisited its story line, I noticed an autobiographically-inspired plot. A man's world turns to shit. The man escapes before it goes *boom*. He lands on his feet in another solar system and becomes something entirely new. Mind you, it's a work in progress, a working title, and my first ever attempt at a novel. But hell, yeah, I'm proud of it.

After writing the novel, I wasn't sure if I would go back to the memoir. Months passed. Maybe I should develop the sci-fi into a limited series? I still might do that. But the memoir, the story of my past life, pestered me to write about it. My mind needed to return to the scene of the crash, to rummage through the debris. I felt I had to look for a teddy bear or any proof of a life that was not all bad, a trace of a memory of the joys that had been dwarfed by all the sorrows.

Picking through this rubble is perhaps what this present book is all about. It's an opportunity to salvage a life full of tender moments from the smoldering debris of a failed flight of fancy. A marriage photo, a loving wife still at my side. Children at an Easter egg hunt. A memento here and one there that are still cherished parts of me.

I don't think it is too far-fetched to paint this picture of a crash site that represents casualties on the ground that did not deserve the calamity that came crashing down around them. As I fell, so to speak, I did my best to land away from others just going about their sacred lives.

The single treasure that I found in the rubble was my own life no longer under the heavy hand of dogma or a fantasy offered by an ancient civilization trying to explain its relative existence.

Absolute obedience was my signature trait throughout my childhood and teens and early adulthood. After I met Alex Klein, I became an enthusiastic volunteer who burst onto the scene and into the kingdom portrayed by the Gospel. My confidence in a spiritual source informed my life for two decades while I observed and resisted the status quo of the old Church's dogma. It was during that time in my life that I learned to trust my own instincts and think on my own. In this manner, I gained confidence in my own powers of reasoning and learned that I could depart from a denomination that no longer satisfied my new vision.

While I actively experienced this growth in the Church, the result was an inner realization that led me to a hunger and thirst for righteousness. For the truth. This hunger set me to turning over stones in pursuit of knowledge. Asking questions. Questioning authority. Considering what others had learned from the same Scripture. I acknowledged their diversity of thought, but also reserved a place for my own conclusions. Forever grateful to Alex Klein, who opened my eyes, I took this curiosity with me and applied it to a new, secular world. I would miss our times together and mourned the fact that what we had once was no longer mutual and, since his passing, is no longer possible.

I am a *Homo sapiens*. My dad knew that, though he preferred the term "wise ass." (I reserve the same label for those I cherish the most.) I relish how unique and promising our species is on its own with no myth needed to explain why we exist or how we've come to exist. Our capacity for empathy and love, to nurture, to hope, does not originate in an unseen deity. I do not exist on this earth as the result of some divine belch moving over sacred dust or clay. Or can I salvage the word "sacred"? Perhaps the stardust from which molecules scampered and formed the primordial life that blossomed to become me are in fact sacred—sacred to me and born out of my new understanding of what it means to be human. The miracle of life is something sacred to me. The gift of life, my grasp of it, even a mortal life on the clock, is wondrous. From my expansive overlook, I claim the right to call all the wonder that my new outlook encompasses, *sacred*. In that context, this word is as profound to me as it was when I used it to describe the divine.

29

Regrets

What's that saying about spilled tea...or was it milk?

Nature or nurture—which influenced the person in the mirror more? My wife often reminds me that I am who I am because of the Church, how it shaped me, and how I gravitated to its teachings and the men I had emulated as heroes in that life. She's right, of course. Nothing shaped me more in my earlier life than the teachings of the Church and my parents.

Whatever qualms I might have had back in those days, I accept my part, including the self-deception. I hid away my doubts. I was concerned I'd disappoint those I loved, afraid to explore the facts that I kept in that room between my ears. That said, I cannot ignore the genuine dedication and sacrifice I proffered while I was fully engaged for the cause. The idea that I never believed, or that I was a wolf in sheep's clothing, is preposterous.

When I consider any of the regrets I have, I remind myself that somewhere during that trek I became a responsible adult. For the balance of my sixty years of life, my self-worth was determined by the Christian tapestry hanging on the wall of my Platonic cave.

While attending Cerritos College, I had watched young people napping through their peak years, so after I graduated, I challenged myself to make up for lost time and signed up for sailing lessons. Although Joe and other ministers golfed regularly, I preferred sailing, which was always a dream when I was younger. I was about to find out what I'd missed.

Our sailing instruction began in the classroom. Once we had those lessons on board, we headed down to the docks. One thing the instructor emphasized dockside came in handy just minutes later. Remembering earlier days, I relived the dreaded rituals of team choosing. Each boat would have a pair of students, and it was obvious nobody wanted to get paired with the old guy. Once it was determined who drew that short straw, we were told to pick a boat. Life jackets were adjusted, and, fortunately, I boarded the fourteen-foot Catalina sailboat first. I placed my hand on the mast and calculated the best place to put my foot. Oops, wrong place. The boat tipped. Trying my best to right the shifting hull beneath my feet, I remembered the instructions our teacher had given, knowing immediately they were most likely emphasized for the big guy (me). Letting go of the mast, I let the weight of my body take me into the cold water. In one fell swoop, I sent all the other boats a-bobbing, fodder for the kids choking back their laughter.

Remembering to let go of the mast before the boat damaged any of the other craft nearby probably saved me from having to call my insurance agent that day. Free of the misplaced ballast, the boat righted itself. I learned how not to board a sailboat. Yes, I was the eldest in the group by a significant factor, and I had to accept, once again, the reality of my life and the things that had passed me by during my youth. Still, I felt proud when I got my certification. I was hooked by the sport.

Soon after the class ended, I became the owner of a 505 sailboat in disrepair. She was a sleek racing craft designed for youth or pristine bodies of any age. I dreamed of salt spray and racing buoys as I labored to give her a new life, but I didn't come close to breaking-even after I sold her to a group of eager friends, who told me to join them anytime, knowing at one glance that I would not. I'd had a great childhood despite not being able to learn to sail. Everything is relative, and I learned a while back that happiness depends on appreciating what you have. Gratitude and mindfulness are key factors in this life.

To be clear about my precious teen years, my father and most leaders considered such adventures as temptations or time drains that limited my time to serve the Lord. He frowned on careers that might have taken me to exotic places. My desires to become a backwoods forest ranger, a fighter pilot, or a thoracic surgeon, those I obediently burned on the altar as a sacrifice of my will. Then, when the NAC ordained a medical doctor as an Apostle, I scratched my head. He was my age and from Canada. How was that even possible? Not one of my mentors, family or otherwise, ever pointed to any options that would have presented me with the same opportunities.

When I visit my regrets now, I understand what a waste of time living in the past can be. I relish living in the present, enjoying my freedom and the richness of family and nature, hence the sailing lessons. It is a waste of time to blame the adults who poured me into their mold. But, alas, I am guilty of the same sin relative to my own children's upbringing.

I did a lot of packing and unpacking as I examined where, and how, I had invested my youth; time that I'd never get back. It was a matter of focusing on the fun I had with many friends, including my wife whom I met in the youth group. It was not all bad, and there are plenty of lessons from my past which I find useful today and can be applied to life, either in or out of the Church. I have found logical answers to replace all the religiously saturated life hacks of the past. It is possible to navigate life without a god.

My belief that there is no hereafter allows for just one scenario. As a species, we have evolved from a chaotic sequence of events, our bits originating from stardust, those tiny building blocks coalescing into more complex bits and then—*poof*, we're returned to dust. Is that all there is? I had it right as a minister: "ashes to ashes, dust to dust." And if I had left it at that, I would have covered it all.

From our perch atop the food chain, (unless we wander naively off into the Serengeti, alone, without a gun and the survival skills we'd need), I'd venture to say we have the best view of the situation. We're born, we die. Others like us continue making stuff, including more of us. Rinse and repeat. So it may not make a lot of difference how we spend this life, whether in an ingrown philosophical cave or in a tower made of books. Or does it? When we're recycled, the bits that gave us the ability to observe life and its constant cycle of life and death, those bits that allowed us to record that knowledge, will all cease to function. Oh, dear, I'm just making it sound so philosophical. Try this one: when our brain rots, it can't do shit anymore. None of us will survive death or be able to say, "Told ya so!" So what's the use?

But I do feel a much deeper sense of being now than I had before, when life after death was still in the picture. I see a past, layered and profound, whether I consider my own children or a stranger's kid playing in a remote part of our world. I see our kind taking the hand of another, taking the baton, and setting out to hand it off. Stepping out of myself and taking in the diversity of our species, I see a thread woven through the chaos and an increasing ability to appreciate our capabilities. For as many who are crippled by fear and ignorance, there are enough dreamers and explorers filled with curiosity and focused on new frontiers and patiently prodding the universe for solutions to the threats underfoot. Within our society, there lies a reservoir of intelligence that comes together unselfishly to consider future generations. The soldier that takes a bullet for the cause. The nerd that forgoes superhero status to crunch numbers, also for the cause. And what is that cause if not the whole? Our habitat. Every biological system pertaining to life. The almost certain promise of life beyond our solar system. The assembling of dreams into tangible steps leading to leaps that lead to knowledge that leads to answers. Verifiable answers about everything, which we record meticulously for posterity. And let's not forget the countless errors and sacrifices made in the name of progress. What do you think this book is about, anyway?

Back in my reality now, I still have to wonder if it would have made any difference if my parents had read the alternatives to the Ten Commandments proffered by Bertrand Russell (1872-1970), rather than those of Moses. And then made use of Russell's commandments to examine their lives before I was born. Russell published these for the first time in 1951, a year before my parents were married, in the *New York Times Magazine*. What if they had chosen Russell's advice about authority, especially religious authorities over their parents' authority, a big ask in those days? Maybe yes, but so what? Maybe I could have given my talents to promoting Russell's commandments and offering the world a different option from the one which captured me.

Bertrand Russell's Ten Commandments[1] offer advice that was obviously well thought out. He warns about arriving at absolute conclusions, for instance. My favorite commandment suggests that authorities are a dime a dozen, meaning in my mind that if you don't like what one person in a place of authority offers, then seek your answer elsewhere.

When I came through the looking glass, having examined my life of sacred assumptions, I was glad that I was not standing in open traffic, that I had replaced that old "truth" with a new concept of the natural world I existed in. I was thrilled to have hold of the proof that established my

---

1. Alternatives to the Ten Commandments - Wikipedia

mortality. That became my Truth with a "capital T." It was an honest picture of the universe from whence I came. I can still make it sound all godly if I want to throw in a few thee's and thou's.

But the process I used to compare my old beliefs with the newly acquired knowledge also exposed an abundance of fools, some who had grabbed up great power and bestowed upon themselves the titles and honors of kings. Those fools divided our species into categories. It seems that many of us lined up to be placed in those categories, lazily allowing them to put ideas into our heads.

Religion offered significant benefits to our societal structure and allowed more of us to agree on certain principles, which brought continuity, which made it possible for more of us to live together in harmony. We could form larger communities and larger armies to protect the naive ideas we came up with.

30

Happiness Defined

What floats your boat?

I was glad when she said, "Let's have breakfast on the patio." It was a beautiful spring Sunday morning, one of those moments when I paused to think about those we had once greeted as brothers and sisters and spent our Sundays with. I knew that at that moment they would most likely be in church while Beth and I were enjoying another aspect of our secular life. These moments, some common, others extraordinary, would have never happened on a Sunday because, well, Sunday was for church. Period. A day of rest, of worship, of Christian fellowship.

As we enjoyed a savory Earl Grey sweet roll, I shared my frustration with this book's progress. I was stuck. More and more, I had doubts about the value of sharing my new world view. Pausing to take a sip of some very black coffee, I said to Beth, "You know, I've been thinking that for those that are content not asking too many questions, practicing one's faith really doesn't matter. It really makes little difference in this world. But you'd have to be content ignoring some real-world knowledge which has been available for many years now."

I was thinking about everyone that I once shared that cave with, who still practiced their faith. I was all right with their choice and could not find it in me to criticize them as long as they were truly happy. But now and then the thought would come, "If only I could save them from that life." A life that I was glad I had left behind. And then I remembered the fate of that fella that returned to Plato's cave. They took his life because his message was too much for their ears to hear.

I once heard in a sermon, "It's a wonderful way to live." The preacher was referring to abandoning one's will, to following the instructions of the Church on all matters. Which meant trusting another person to think for you. In this case, a person whose logic was filled with holes. I suppose some people might find it wonderful, not fretting over life's challenges, believing that all the answers are a phone call or a sermon away.

This was only part of my struggle as I considered the opinions and reactions to what I wanted to share with those who came into my thoughts over those tasty, sweet, rolls on that beautiful spring Sunday morning. How would they receive my memoir? How would they react to this book about my life, which was once shared in the same bubble and now transcended their beliefs?

The reason I have continued writing this far, setting this work aside and then taking it up after a few emotionally induced comas, is because I have come across individuals who have experienced religion in a considerably more detrimental way than I did. Perhaps they can right their ship in the storm they're in. I'm here to tell you that there is life on the other side of religion, and it is most satisfying.

I do, however, wrestle in the here-and-now with the potential damage that unbridled religious fervor could bring upon our society. And, by extension, to our home among the stars.

Sunday mornings on the patio are a beautiful way to exercise freedom from religion. So is taking an inventory of your humanity. While in some ways I am who I am because of the Church, I can also still recognize the man that existed despite the brand and ideals once worn. I have set him free to pursue his remaining dreams. Perhaps this is like the woman who looks at herself in a mirror, confident that her mature beauty is so much more than the youthful form she inhabited back in the day. At the same time, she is considering her spouse, who has left her, believing he can recapture his youth vicariously. She gave her younger self to him, only to find him inadequate. Sometimes I'm left feeling this way as I think about the promise of religion, one that failed to deliver for me in my golden years, whose promise of eternal life crumbled under closer scrutiny. Yeah, and robbed me of my youth in order to promote a myth.

Today, my respect for that old myth exists only as an acknowledgment of the ancient civilizations and thinkers, who did the best they could, having so little information about the universe at the time. They could only formulate ideas based on what they were taught and could relate to during their lives. I believe a myth can still serve us if we can extract its wisdom without falling for the supernatural aspects carried over from the uninformed, aka, the wise men of that past era.

Crediting a mythical being as the source of our wisdom, rather than the miracle we experience as an advanced species, is an error we need to make haste to correct. Humility aside, the human mind *can* truly become exceptional. We have all stood in awe of the exceptional human being who elegantly illustrates our place and existence in marvelous ways. These giants among us may seem rare, but what of the ones waiting to excel, those shackled by ancient rumors and unfounded lore? Finding gold in a mountain stream can make one rich, and persevering until they make a strike is admirable. But just as one knows that such treasure exists in a formation of stone and earth, so there are other kinds of treasures waiting to be uncovered. Einstein's beautiful mind placed him among photons as they sped through space. This intimate mind experiment with one of the most common elements in our universe provided him with a key to unlock possibilities that most commoners would not have considered. And he is not the only mind that has provided us with a glimpse of genius,

Schrödinger's imaginary cat, another thought experiment, helps a simple mind like mine grasp quantum physics and, specifically, the concept of superposition.

While I know my limitations, I am still astonished by the mind I have escaped with. Consider the fact that over the billions of years that have unfolded, you and I are one among the billions that can grasp the significance of the stars. I know as a matter of fact that the dusty nebula and all its related bits have coalesced naturally and so fashioned us *Homo sapiens* plus every rung on the evolutionary ladder, resulting in our specificity.

I keep walking up to this precipice and considering how easy it was for the thinkers of our species to conjure up the gods. The gods, too, have evolved. This makes perfect sense. All gods, including the most common iterations of our time, have been constructs of our thinking minds. The men that did that conjuring may have been feared or admired, or both. When these curious minds collaborated, comparing similar ideas, the existence of only one God, for instance, the product of their creative minds coalesced into broader and more useful social tools. All of these were based on their illustrious imaginations. Once that ball was rolling, well...that's history. A history shaped by unprovable, speculative constructs which, like pharmaceuticals designed for one purpose, double as an opiate for the masses.

I can appreciate the logic of the monotheistic god. While taking the college course in astrobiology (and while still a believer), I enjoyed considering the singularity from which the Big Bang is said to have sprung. I empathize with the apologist who would accept the creation as science presents it today, but still wants to cling to the idea that a singularity somehow appeared in a true vacuum, set there by the pinched fingers of a petulant, childlike god who bounced in his seat and patted his hands together when the thing actually went *bang!* This is my mind thinking again about how to justify a god.

The one thing I would say is that if God is laughing at me as I write this, in considering my best efforts of trying to understand the universe (to ask how it came to be or any other specific detail is all part of understanding the thing), the most I ought to be accused of is an error in semantics. It is simply hubris to accept or repeat the conclusion of any person who claims to possess such information. This is especially true for those that claim to be spokespersons for such an entity. Building a religion from such a premise is an authentic example of making a mountain out of a molehill. There are far too many molehills posing as mountains in our world.

I have spent much of my adult lifetime convincing myself and others that a supernatural being created us. In a word, since we exist, He must exist. Regardless of the many theological arguments that are used to argue for the existence of an eternal god, *it was my determined conclusion that this being was a construct of the human mind, and nothing more.* As were all the rules and edicts attributed to that being. My conclusion left all pro-god arguments in a heap, erasing that being from my concept of reality.

I can neither confirm nor deny the existence of God. No one can. But my personal belief that God is a product of man's thinking is the key reason I no longer believe in God.

It has become, and remains my opinion, that it may be impossible for us human beings to know for certain how we came to be. That includes any notion of why we exist. Attempting to elevate our existence to some sacred level because it was the best explanation back in the day is so far beyond our capacity as thinkers and or explorers that I count it pure hubris.

I cannot deny the existence of God as a major contributor to world history, and His ongoing presence as an entity in the minds of believers will continue to affect future world history. At some point, when the majority of people welcomed Him to the world stage and accepted His God-head; that conjured presence became an unstoppable force shaping the minds and ideals of all future believers and potentates. And, yes, some good found its way into our world. The world needs such good notions if for nothing else than to help us humans discover that goodness lies at the heart of our future success as a species. But we ought to claim this good as a part of our human legacy, a product of our mental health and education rather than as a religious benefit.

One day, I asked myself what a world without God might look like and initiated my own thought experiment to explore that scenario. Each of life's harsh realities became easier to understand and deal with. Death without reward or judgement was simplified, sickness and tragedy were all deflated and easily understood, shit happens—right? Prayer, when it seemed to work, was more of a fluke than a promise. Before me was an explanation that easily fit my experience. After my thought experiment, after I concluded life made more sense without a deity, I settled into my new world. Exercise and healthy lifestyle choices were tangibles and from there on the only means I had of elbowing back at the existential chaos around me. I had found my new happy place.

I only claim happiness in the here and now. I endure the falling leaves and storms that mark time. My purpose, because it tickles my fancy, is to appreciate beauty and to create beauty as my eye beholds it. To know you, a person, based on how you respond to my creations. I create beauty to mimic the place where I exist, the reach of my eye, the reflection of your joy, your pain. Beauty to me exists wherever I can discover it, whether with the naked eye or through an instrument revealing quantum fuzziness. Or from words carved out of knowledge, experience, and exploration. And if it happens, that one of our kind will lift a finger to point at a verifiable god.

It is my opinion that it will not be the religious believers that agree, but the theorists, the thinkers, and the tinkerers that say *Aha!*

I accept that I can only know some things. That our species will continue to uncover the actual workings of the cosmos. Our species—the whole of us—may not have enough time to learn it all. I do not refer to any looming threat now facing humankind, although threats remain dark possibilities. I refer to big history, the history of the universe, which will record our entire existence and that of our solar system under the point of a pen. A single pinpoint, the time it takes this writer to pause and lift it, moving to write another line, everything we know, every creature that has drawn breath, all the time passed, under that one dot. Relativity, baby!

Meanwhile, on my patio, I will appreciate the view and relish the light that reveals all things beautiful; until the moment it....

Travel safely.

Conclusion

A Final Ripple

Aaron Copeland (1900-1990) wrote a stunning piece of music he called "Fanfare for the Common Man." After I got over myself as a spiritual being trapped in a human experience and accepted my place as a common man, I began to appreciate that the potential for our species, while relatively ordinary, is exceptional in so many ways. Copeland's exceptional music inspired me to reach out after such commonality.

I used to believe that spirituality was a component of our unique status as *Homo sapiens,* translated as "Wise humans." After acknowledging that I no longer believed in any gods, I began to focus on the evolving aspect of being human and the significance of myself as a mortal man whose life is not everlasting.

I now think of the spirituality I once enjoyed as a state of mind. I recently communicated with a person who wanted to enlighten me regarding the *mystical life.* He and those he looked to for metaphysical wisdom wanted to help me believe that an individual's encounter with that side of our humanity can serve as a personal form of empirical evidence and therefore (personal) proof that man is more than the sum of his physical existence. I was not able to either make that leap or to accept the poetic license taken.

After I began to appreciate the benefits of being a non-believer, I wondered (for a short time) if any of life's challenges might bring me to my knees again to pray. As a pastor, I had been with people near death who, after a lifetime of denial or disinterest, now confessed a belief in God and requested absolution. Today, as an unbeliever I am occasionally challenged to work through "new doubt," but then I conclude that I am not in danger of relapsing. After considering how I felt at the height of my spiritual enthusiasm, which was bordering on a state of mystical bliss, and considering the personal "empirical evidence" I possessed at that time, I concluded that what I was feeling was equivalent to a state of mind. It was the same state of mind a child might achieve after stumbling into a hiding place in the woods, perhaps a hollow in a thicket of brush left by a large animal, a place to hide, to feel safe and aloof.

And so it is as I continue down my new path. Such a state of mind no longer holds the ethereal comfort it once did, nor do I miss it.

I suspect that all religions will eventually go the way of the *Cro Magnon*, and in the process, reveal that *Homo sapiens* have plenty of wisdom. They (we) only need to foster it to survive without a god.

We also crave attention and notoriety. As a boy, I watched as my siblings and cousins frantically put together plays for our parents, digging in a toy box for props worthy of their creativity and all produced within a short timetable. I only watched, not being drawn into the pageantry, but still yearning to be noticed. Team building was not something I experienced growing up. It was in my nature to fly solo for whatever reason. But the desire to have some social connection, to take part for the benefit of the whole, has prompted me to share what I have learned in moments of quiet contemplation, the one thing I cherish most.

I believe in passion. I happen to have many passions, and from passions proceed ripples that move across time. Sharing knowledge is a passion of mine. I hope my ripple in time finds you prosperous and whole, your own passion enlivening your soul, refreshing your smiles, and diminishing your tears so that you can truly recognize the beautiful being that you are.

Acknowledgements

I began this project alone, intending to share a few stories about my life as a gift for my kids, something that they could tease me about, and have as a keepsake. When I expanded the idea, deciding instead to write a memoir, an entire village came to my aid. There is a cabal of writers and authors who magnanimously share their expertise online. Without that collective generosity, I would still be wandering about with no book in hand.

This book exists because of the generous help provided at home, right from the start and through the four years of rewrites and, finally, the last slog to publishing day.

Dear Beth, you and I lived the life portrayed in this memoir–hand in hand. I am so thankful for your patience and guidance. My need to complete this required that both of us relive both the triumphs and challenges of that period in our life. I'm happy to say that we survived the process and much more. This memoir would not have materialized without your wisdom and amazing patience.

To my children Sarah, Leah, Will and Tobe, your presence off-stage, as I traveled back in time, was always a reminder that you too lived this life. Each step I took through our shared experience reminded me how valuable your love remains to me. We may not all appreciate where my journey took me, but my heart will always be there for each one of you. I will always love and respect you and your families.

To my dear niece Lindsay, thank you for wading through my first "final" (now archived) draft, and for your inspiration and support. Your advice was spot on and just what I needed to hear.

Dad, part of you lives on in me. It was your attempt to write a memoir which lit a fire under the man you and mom raised.

Mom, had you not rescued Dad's "opus", it's possible this book would have never existed. The butterfly's wing in action. I cherish your influence on my life, your whispers and laughs that shaped who I became.

To my editor, Barbara Ardinger, Ph.D. You took my project on and provided the polish I lacked as a newbie writer. Barbara, I am glad we met that day at the California Writer's Club.

As our fraternity's Chief Apostate, Lon Ostrander, befriended me and welcomed me as a fellow into the Clergy Project. His willingness to write my foreword and lend his shared experience to my story was a noble gift and much appreciated. Thank you, sir.

Nick Overduin, Ph.D. Such a kindness you've shared. Your willingness to be one of my first readers remains flattering, which then you expanded with your expert comments and review of my manuscript. I look forward to your memoir. You certainly have the skills!

Christina Lozonski, what a keen mind you've lent me. Your contribution was invaluable: Prescient finishing touches that only fresh eyes could provide. Merci beaucoup.

Tom Brower, your review of the pre-edited draft provided just the right amount of praise and subjective perspective needed as I worked out the bugs. I can't thank you enough!

So many people have answered the call, giving their advice and help, their encouragement and council. To my readers on Medium.com I thank you for your comments and claps. Observers from several platforms have cheered me on sharing their time and knowledge which helped me carry on.

Many have entered my life and left their mark; some are no longer with us. The villages and congregations we have called home, the well-meant wisdom and criticism tendered, all shaped who I became. I am fortunate to have had such friends in this life.

And to those of you willing to take a chance on a new author, I thank you. I hope my story offered some measure of comfort and help on your journey.

Thank You

Thank you for reading -Go and Preach No More-.

I hope you enjoyed reading my memoir. I guess if you've come this far, there's a good chance that's true. Please consider rating and reviewing my book using the QR code at the back of this book.

You can also follow me on my Facebook page. (See the QR codes at the back of this book – they replace the clickable links available in the eBook version.)

I also write on Medium.com. Email me and request a friend link. It will allow you past the paywall to read my stories.

If you would like to get in touch with me, please email me at this address: Bill@wmraff.com. I'm always interested in hearing what readers have to say. And, I'm always looking for beta-readers to help me in the writing process. Your feedback is priceless. Beta-readers get free copies of new books and play an important role in getting good books published.

I still have many stories to tell. Some, about my passion for woodworking, which has always been a part of me. Another, an introspective into brotherhood, as a tribute to my late brother, John.

I also have a first draft completed for a science-fiction novel, all of which will need some eager beta readers.

But for now, farewell.

P.S. Reminder, you'll find a page of QR-Codes at the end of the Appendices. Use the camera on your mobile phone and the QR codes to go directly to all the links on this page and the entire books.

Appendix 1

Plato's Allegory of the Cave

The Republic - Book 7

Source: https://pressbooks.library.torontomu.ca/republic/

This allegory is quite lengthy, and often offered as a synopsis. I have included a link if you want to read it in its entirety. This copy is available in several formats and free to download. It has no copyright restrictions according to the source.

This is the text of the first page as written in The Republic, by Plato, where Socrates is telling the story, and Glaucon, Plato's brother, is answering:

***

"And now, I said, let me show in a figure how far our nature is enlightened or unenlightened:—Behold! human beings living in an underground den, which has a mouth open towards the light and reaching all along the den; here they have been from their childhood, and have their legs and necks chained so that they cannot move, and can only see before them, being prevented by the chains from turning round their heads. Above and behind them, a fire is blazing at a distance, and between the fire and the prisoners there is a raised way; and you will see, if you look, a low wall built along the way, like the screen which marionette players have in front of them, over which they show the puppets."

"I see."

"And do you see, I said, men passing along the wall carrying all sorts of vessels, and statues and figures of animals made of wood and stone and various materials, which appear over the wall? Some of them are talking, others silent."

"You have shown me a strange image, and they are strange prisoners."

"Like ourselves," I replied, "and they see only their own shadows, or the shadows of one another, which the fire throws on the opposite wall of the cave?"

"True," he said; "how could they see anything but the shadows if they were never allowed to move their heads?"

"And of the objects which are being carried in like manner they would only see the shadows?"

"Yes," he said.

"And if they were able to converse with one another, would they not suppose that they were naming what was actually before them?"

"Very true." (I made some minor grammatical changes to what I copied and pasted.)

***

One synopsis, as I remember my professor telling it, describes an individual drawn to the natural light outside the den, or cave. He escapes. Once outside the cave, that person is enlightened about the facts regarding his experience and realizes that the shadows which previously made up their concept of reality had been fabricated.

Armed with this knowledge, they reenter the cave to share this news with those they were once shackled with the intention to free them all. The prisoners, however, prefer their version of truth, and take that person's life.

Appendix 2

- <u>A Fifty-Nine-Year Timeline of my Christian Life</u>

- <u>1953 - 1963 Age 0 - 10</u>

- 1953 I was born in June. We lived on Coringa Dr. Highland Park, Los Angeles, CA.

- I was baptized with water and the Holy Spirit, becoming a member of the New Apostolic Church, Highland Park congregation shortly after birth.

- 1955 My brother John was born in July.

- 1956 We moved to Sycamore Dr. Los Angeles, CA.

- 1957 My sister Jennie was born in March.

- 1958 My parents bought our first home on Rangeview Avenue Los Angeles, CA.

- 1958-1963 Attended Buchanan Elementary.

- <u>1964 - 1974 Age 11 - 21</u>

- 1963-1964 My parents bought our second home on Roy Street,

Los Angeles, CA.

- 1964-1966 Attended Garvanza Elementary.

- 1966 Michael Kraus was assigned to the USA. He was 58 yrs old.

- 1966-1969 Attended Luther Burbank Junior High.

- Spring 1968 My Confirmation, which adds youth activities to my schedule.

- 1969-1971 Attended Benjamin Franklin High.

- 1969-1970 Worked as a box boy at Boy's Market in Highland Park.

- 1971 Graduated High School in June.

- 1971-1972 Attended Glendale Community College.

- 1971-1973 Joined Carpenter's Apprentice Program - Worked as an apprentice carpenter. Attended night classes at Los Angeles Trade Tech as part of my training.

- 1971 Oct. 17 I was ordained as a sub-deacon by D-Ap.M. Kraus.

- 1973 Kraus turned 65 and should have retired.

- 1974 Apr. 28 I was ordained as a deacon by D-Ap.M. Kraus

- 1974 Worked P/T delivering blueprints to/from architects in the Wilshire/Downtown L.A. area.

- 1974 Worked as a freelance carpenter.

- 1974 Met Beth at a choir practice in Pasadena, CA.

- <u>1975-1985 Age 22 - 32</u>

- 1975 First missionary trip to Guam with Bill Uhl. 2 weeks. We were both deacons.

- 1975 Started apprenticeship as an industrial pattern maker at Apex Pattern, Los Angeles, CA.

- 1976 Continued Apprenticeship at Practical Pattern Shop. Los Angeles, CA.

- 1978 Married Beth on Dec 3rd.

- 1979 Transferred to Whittier, CA Congregation as an assistant Priest.

- 1979 June 24-Ordained as Priest by Ap. E. Wagner.

- 1979 Purchased our house in June - Moved there in September.

- 1979 Sarah was born in November. (1st child/daughter)

- 1979-80 Transferred to Anaheim congregation.

- 1981 July 26 - Assigned to be the rector of Anaheim by Ap. E. Wagner.

- 1981 Leah was born in September (daughter)

- 1983 William T. was born in September (son)

- 1983 September - Alex Klein becomes District Elder for West Coast.

- 1984 June 17-Ordination as Evangelist by Ap. W. Vovak.

- 1985 First missionary trips to Mexico begin. - Ap. J. Fendt was in charge of Mexico.

- <u>1986 - 1996 Age 33 - 43</u>

- 1986 June. Leonard Kolb Sr. Ordained Apostle and commissioned D. Ap. Helper.

- 1986 June. Leonard Kolb Sr. is assigned the California and Mexico Districts

- 1987 Alex Klein Ordained Bishop in May.

- 1989 Tobit is born (son)

- 1989 November. I buyout Andy Hazell and take over as President of Practical Pattern Shop, Inc.

- 1990 February. John's death - car accident. (brother)

- 1990 Summer - PPS, Inc. begins dba Glasslines. Move John's business into vacant building /Slauson property. Dad continues as our salesperson. Oliver runs production.

- 1990 Break-ins start in September at Slauson shop / Storage container.

- 1991 Sent Oliver to rehab.

- 1991 Shut down Glasslines.

- 1990 Recession takes its toll on shop / Andy Hazell let go.

- 1993 Started courses in CAD-CAM & CNC at NHTMA

- 1994 Kraus finally retires at 87 yrs old. Wagner becomes District Apostle for North America.

- 1995 Nov.- Began conversion of pattern shop from conventional mfg. to CAD-CAM-CNC technology.

- 1996 Jan. Haas VF-2 CNC machine goes into service.

- 1996 June. Moved shop to Lakeland Ave, Santa Fe Springs, CA. I mile from home.

- <u>1997 - 2007 Age 44 - 54</u>

- 2000 Richard Freund is ordained in May as District Apostle for the U.S. in Pasadena.

- 2001 Michael Kraus' death at the age of 95.

- 2002. NAC National Synod / Chicago, ILL. September 27-28.

- 2003 Leonard Kolb Sr. retired in May; Len Kolb Jr. took over L.A. District.

- 2003 Alex Klein retires Oct 26.

- 2004 My Retirement after 26 years of ministry at 51 yrs old - Nov 28.

- 2005 We Started attending FAFC in January.

- 2006 Midterm elections. Democrats take a majority in the House.

- 2006 or beginning of 2007 Inquiry into becoming a minister, intending to attend Life Pacific University.

- 2007 Spring - Began attending Cerritos College to complete AA in preparation to transfer to Life Pacific.

- 2007 Albert and Sarah moved to Colorado Springs. July.

- 2007 Began part time position as small group coordinator at FAFC. October.

- <u>2008 - 2012 Age 55 - 59</u>

- 2008 Sailing Lessons at OCC school of sailing. May-June.

- 2008 Bought a boat trailer with a free 505 sailboat included. July.

- 2008 Completed AA degree at Cerritos College. June.

- 2008 Obama wins the presidential election that November.

- 2009 Passed the test for the General Contractor License. March.

- 2009 Received General Contractors License / The Green Craftsman Inc. (formerly P.P.S. Inc.)

- 2008-2010 rebuilt the boat trailer and the 505 sailboat.

- 2010 September - Dad's crisis event, which signaled the last days of his battle with Alzheimer's.

- 2010 Last year at FAFC / stayed through Christmas, began visiting other churches in January 2011.

- Mar 15, 2011, Dad passed away.

- Mar 12, 2011, My last prescription for an antidepressant.

- 2011 April-July We started attending Paznaz with friends while attending as podrishioner's at Greg Boyd's church - St. Paul, Minn.

- 2012 January I was finished with organized religion and accepted that I was an atheist.

Appendix 3

Ministries of the New Apostolic Church ~ circa 2004:

Apostolic Ministries:

- Chief Apostle

- District Apostle

- District Apostle Helper (A designation used for organizational purposes only)

- Apostle

Priestly Ministries:

- Bishop

- District Elder

- District Evangelist

- Shepherd

- Evangelist

- Rector (Any priestly ministry designated as the lead minister of a single congregation.)

- Priest

<u>Diaconal Ministries:</u>

- Deacon

- Sub-deacon

(The NAC has since changed, and the entire hierarchy was reduced to include only four primary ministries. Chief Apostle, Apostle, Priest and Deacon. Another system is used to designate responsibility at different levels of the church. i.e. Countries, States, Cities, Congregations)

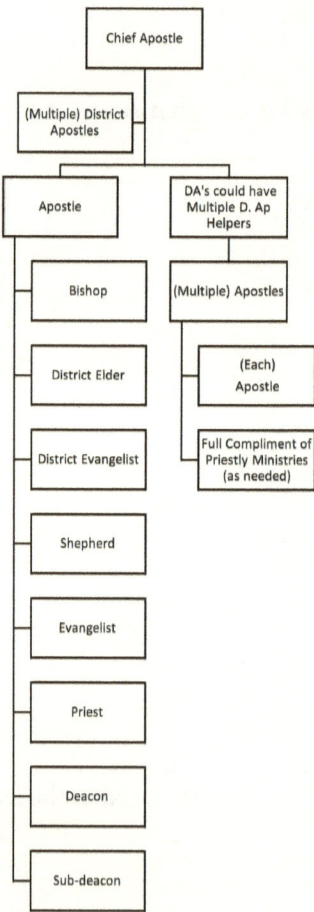

Appendix 4

How the New Apostolic Church -NAC- came to exist:

There are far more detailed accounts of the years, beginning in 1830, that established the Church I grew up in. The international seat of the NAC has an extensive website (Nak.org) that provides detailed information about its beginnings and their current catechism.

During the 1830s in London and Glasgow U.K., various individuals, hopeful that the Holy Spirit would guide them to reanimate their congregations, began holding daily meetings to pray and read the scriptures seeking guidance. Soon, several of them received spiritual gifts similar to those noted in the Gospels. Some spoke in tongues, some had visions, and others prophesied. This led them to establish a congregation in London and call themselves the Catholic Apostolic Church (CAC). Through prophecies, some of these men were called to be apostles for the end time; convincing them that Christ's second coming was imminent.

In 1860, the congregation in Hamburg, Germany, separated from that group, calling themselves the New Apostolic Church.

The CAC, unwilling to allow more than twelve apostles, even though the prophets had called others to be apostles, failed to grow.

The NAC accepted the prophecies and prospered, spreading worldwide.

Appendix 5

Eschatology of the NAC (The doctrine of future events)

The New Apostolic Church from its inception declared its purpose in a very clear and concise way. God had sent living apostles, again, to prepare humanity for the end times. Specifically, the second coming and or the rapture.

During my childhood, the keyword used to refer to that event was *the First Resurrection*. The Bible references several other events that will take place in succession after Christ's return. Theologians refer to this as eschatology, the doctrine of future events.

The eschatology of the NAC stated that those that God considered worthy from among the living and dead in Christ would rise to meet Him in the clouds and proceed to heaven. The living, remnant of the Church, would be spared a natural death. The group taken to Heaven was also referred to as "The hundred and forty-four thousand" (Rev. 14:1-5), the Firstlings, the Bride of Christ and the Overcomers. (For most of my life the church stressed that participation in the rapture was only possible if a soul experienced salvation, by "the laying on of hands of a living apostle" (also known as the rebirth of water and spirit in the NAC).

The NAC has now modified its opinion to say: "Whether God will also grant the grace of the rapture to others is beyond human judgement and is subject to the decision of God." The Catechism in Questions & Answers – New Apostolic Church International

Christians — left behind — would need to prove themselves during a Great Tribulation on the earth during which Satan would prey on those remaining and cause untold destruction of the physical world.

Meanwhile, in heaven, the marriage of the Lamb would be taking place. (Christ - married to those taken into heaven). After which, Christ would return with His bride to reign on earth for a period called the thousand years of peace. This would allow time for all souls who had ever walked the earth, living or dead, to hear about the gospel of Christ and accept it. Then, the last judgment would take place, the good granted everlasting life, and the evil condemned to everlasting death. And finally, God would create a new heaven and a new earth.

Future events list:

- The Rapture followed by the marriage of the Lamb of God.

- On earth, during the festivities in heaven: an unspecified time of tribulation.

- Christ returns to earth with his bride and a thousand years of peace begins on earth.

- The Last Judgment.

- God creates a new heaven and a new earth.

Official NAC/NAK catechism on future events

Appendix 6

History of The Clergy Project

First Awareness

In 2006, just before The God Delusion was released, Dan Barker met with Richard Dawkins at the annual Humanist conference in Reykjavik, Iceland. During the conference, Dawkins listened with great interest as Barker shared his preacher-to-atheist story. He was deeply moved by the plight of non-believing clergy and expressed his desire to find a way to help these men and women. However, at that time, a viable solution did not present itself. Later, when Dawkins wrote the foreword to Barker's book Godless: How an Evangelical Preacher Became One of America's Leading Atheists, he remembered their conversation, and again shared his desire to assist non-believing clergy.

Barker, being a former minister who lost his faith, was well acquainted with the plight of non-believing clergy. For more than two decades, he had met numerous religious leaders who had lost their faith. With their permission, he documented their stories. His desire to assist these clergy persons never waned, but the solution was still out of reach. Bruce Grierson included Barker's and other non-believing ministers' stories in an article he wrote for Psychology Today. (February 2008 issue)

The Role of Academic Research

Philosopher Daniel Dennett and researcher Linda LaScola conducted a study, published in the March 2010 issue of Evolutionary Psychology, entitled, "Preachers Who Are Not Believers." Dan Barker assisted them in finding three of the five original participants. There were 30 additional participants in a follow-up book, "Caught in the Pulpit: Leaving Belief Behind", that was published in May 2013 with an expanded and updated edition released in 2015. Dennett and LaScola's hard work, as well as the active clergy who participated in the study, are vital components in the creation of The Clergy Project. (NOTE: Since neither Dennett nor LaScola are current or former ministers, they are not TCP participants and do not participate in the Online Community.)

The Launch – March 20, 2011

Like a 'perfect storm', each of the encounters above coalesced into what is now The Clergy Project (TCP). An acting Board of Directors was formed, and they developed Bylaws, applied for and were Incorporated as a Non-profit in the State of Florida as The Clergy Project, Inc.

The Clergy Project Online Community formally launched on March 20, 2011, with 52 Charter Participants drawn from Dan Barker's interactions with non-believing clergy and participants in the LaScola/Dennett study. Dawkins had provided the necessary funding to develop and launch the TCP Online Community while two non-believing clergy persons going by the names "Adam" and "Chris" helped design the website and served as its very first members.

The purpose from the beginning was to provide a safe, online haven for both current and former non-believing religious leaders. This goal was established through a private Online Community. At the Online Community participants may safely discuss issues freely including the following: being a clergy person who has rejected the supernatural, family stresses related to their rejection of the supernatural, cognitive dissonance, and the unique difficulties of leaving a career as a religious leader.

The Clergy Project's public website went online in October 2011, followed by a public Facebook Page later that same month. https://clergyproject.org/

Appendix 7

Recipes

Grandma Kroner's Streuselkuchen

aka Apfel streuselkuchen (Apple Streusel Cake)

Ingredients:

Dough:

1 stick of butter

¾ cups sugar

2 eggs

3 tsps. Lemon extract

2 cups flour

2 ½ tsps. baking powder

Apples:

1 21 oz can of Comstock brand sliced apples, sliced thin (not pie filling) – (no longer available)

Beth uses 8 fresh (granny smith but any will work) apples–sliced thin–cooked for 5 minutes in a small amount of water

Streusel:

2 sticks butter

1 cup sugar

3 tsps. Lemon extract.

2 cups flour

Streusel topping:

Combine ingredients until butter pieces are pea size, using a pastry blender or 2 butter knives. Set aside.

Cake:

Cream butter and sugar well. Beat in eggs and extract until blended. Combine flour and baking powder. Add flour/baking powder mixture alternately with the milk-half at a time- until blended. Spread into 2–8-inch cake pans or 1 10 in x 14 in sheet pan. Top with rows of apples. Cover with streusel topping. Bake at 350 for 25 to 35 minutes. Cake should be done in center and lightly browned.

***

Gigi's (Beth's) Coffee Cake

Every Christmas since Beth and I were married, she has made this delightful treat for our family. As our children grew up and moved out, she made sure that each Christmas they would get one to share with their families. This recipe was handed down by her dad's mom, Grandma Denning.

Dough:

1 ½ c milk, warmed

½ c sugar

½ c butter, softened or melted

1 tsp vanilla (optional)

2 pkgs. Or 2 Tbsps. Dry yeast.

2 eggs

6-7 c flour

In mixing bowl, pour in milk, sprinkle sugar over, add butter and vanilla. Sprinkle yeast on top and let stand for about 10 minutes for the yeast to dissolve. Add eggs and 5 cups of flour. Mix with dough hook (or by hand), adding extra flour until it forms a ball of dough. Place in greased bowl, turn over once. Cover; let rise in a warm place till double, 1-1 ½ hours. Punch down and divide into two pieces.

Roll each portion out on a floured surface to a large rectangle (approx. 13 x 20). Brush generously with melted butter (1/4 c or more), then sprinkle with sugar (1/4-1/2 cup). Sprinkle generously with cinnamon, then top with chopped pecans (or walnuts if you prefer) and raisins (1/4-1/2 cup each).

Starting from the longest side, roll up like a jellyroll. Place on a greased baking pan/cookie sheet curving in the shape of a ring or oval. With scissors, snip 3/4 of the way to the center at about 1-inch intervals. Rotate/twist each section slightly to one side. Brush the entire coffee cake with melted butter (about ¼ c) Sprinkle top with streusel (1 stick butter, ½ c flour, ¼ c sugar mixed with fork until crumbly-should be enough for both coffee cakes)

Let rise until double, 45-60 minutes. Bake at 375 degrees for 20 -25 minutes until lightly browned. When cool, drizzle with powdered sugar icing (powdered sugar and a little milk and vanilla (optional) until drizzling consistency).

QR Codes for Book Links

Sometimes links change. The author has no control over this.
Apologies if they no longer work. Functioning as of 11/2024

Recovering
from Religion

Alternative
Ten
Commandments

Medium.com

NAK.org

www.wmraff.com

Plato's Cave

FB Page

The Clergy
Project.org

Bill@

Review This
Book Now

About the Author

William Raff is a former minister and Christian whose debut memoir, "Go and Preach No More" portrays a curious man's sixty-year journey alongside a God he would eventually abandon.

Predestined to a life of ministry in a unique church, he earned his living in a secular world. To do this, he would combine his entrepreneurial chutzpah with a fondness for woodworking and enter an equally unique vocation... Becoming a multi skilled, blue-collar philosopher.

As a teen, the demands of his religious upbringing forged his keen ability to tell a story, which he honed for over twenty-five years while delivering thousands of extemporaneous sermons in both the English and Spanish languages.

Naturally creative, Bill's love of music, art and design enhances his ability to appreciate life from many points of view. When his late father's attempt at an autobiography tickled his talent to write, it was one more tool which he discovered felt like an old friend in his hand. His writing style is as unique as his profound understanding of life. His insights and life experience provide a colorful palette, which he has used here to paint his own self-portrait...

He is a native of Southern California where he lives with Beth, his wife of forty-five years.

www.ingramcontent.com/pod-product-compliance
Lightning Source LLC
Chambersburg PA
CBHW021215130626
46554CB00004B/1230